The World's Dimes

or

God's Dollars

Wendy,

May you see God's
faithfulness above all. Jeremiah 29:11

Jennifer Combs

The World's Dimes

or

God's Dollars

Which are you seeking?

~

GeriAnn Combs

 Potter's Publishing
"Like Clay" in the hands of the potter,
so are you in My hands."
(Jeremiah 18:6)

The World's Dimes or God's Dollars

Edited by Joan Britton
Cover design by Theda Llewellyn
Interior designed by Julie Glynn

Published by The Potter's Publishing
"Like Clay" in the hands of the potter, so are you in My hands.
(Jeremiah 18:6)

For information contact:
Potter's Publishing
P.O. Box 174
2582 S. Maguire Rd.
Ocoee, Florida 34761
www.potterspublishing.com

POTTER'S
Publishing

Library of Congress Cataloging-in-Publication Data

ISBN:0-9745810-0-3

Dedication

This book is for the ladies,
who are going through life's tough valleys,
And would like the encouragement from
one who has been there.

Acknowledgements

My heart is full of love and gratitude for my encourager friend Ruth Berkes. If it had not been for her loving nudges over this past decade, there were times when I would have wanted to quit. It was Ruth who first knew our Lord wanted this story written. She never gave up on me! With her encouragement we saw God work in miraculous ways and experienced many victories on this journey. Ruth has spent many hours proof reading this manuscript; She let me know when I went too soft as she had been there praying me through the struggles and pain. She truly is one of God's most precious jewels in my life.

A special acknowledgement goes to my new friend Joan Britton, who had only retired from the mission field a few months ago after forty years of editing and writing with TransWorld Radio, when she felt God's leading to edit this book. Our Lord surprised us both as He put us together at just the right time. The first draft and the last draft of this book are astonishingly different, thanks to several who gave feedback, but it was Joan who had edited not just the first draft, but all subsequent drafts as well. Editors do their work invisibly, but Joan's contributions are very visible to me as I read the final result.

To the man in my life, my husband Richard, whom God has given to complete me, I say a special thank you. He has been patient during the long hours it has taken to complete this book. Thank you for believing in me and cheering me on as you rolled up your sleeves, doing whatever you could to help. Your contributions have been, and continue to be, extremely helpful. Richard's talents shine where mine do not (on the computer to name one.) ☺ I love you, Sweetheart.

I especially want to thank my Lord, for without His faithfulness, His love, care and grace on this journey, there would be no story to tell. But because of it, I MUST tell it for His Glory.

Contents

Introduction

The year was 2001. It was a beautiful August morning in Orlando, Florida. I was sitting in church listening to the beautiful hymns and praise music before the message. Then, out of the blue, God spilled into my mind things that were to be in this book. At first I was stunned, although I had known for several years that I was to write it and had been waiting for God's leading on when to begin. Now I could feel His spirit saying, "The time to start writing is here, my child." Goose bumps came all over me. I could feel a cool breeze gently surrounding me.

Tears of joy filled my eyes as I began writing as fast as I could, hardly able to keep up with what God was giving me. God had given me the title seven years earlier. Then one morning, about two years ago during my quiet time with Him, God had also given me the titles for seven chapters. At that time, I had thought the book would end with chapter 7, "The Dollar—God." But then, just before God said, "It's time to get started on the assignment that I have given to you," He surprised me with the title for the 8th chapter. This chapter is about God's Grace and my "heart's desire."

The following Sunday morning, the same urgent feeling came over me along with the goose bumps. "Write something down for this book," I heard in my spirit. This time, it was short and to the point: "Tell them about your journey and encourage them with theirs."

I look back to my years in Knoxville, Tennessee. God knew that during those years and for some years to come, I would need a good "encourager friend." He gave me Ruby. She told me one day in 1994, she could see how God was leading me as He had led Ruth in the Bible. Ruth didn't know where she was going, or how to get there, but God led her.

The book of Ruth is a story of God's grace in the midst of difficult circumstances. Ruth loved her mother-in-law Naomi so much that she wanted to go with her wherever she went. Naomi's life had been a powerful witness to the reality of God. Ruth was drawn to her and to the God she worshipped. (I pray He will use me too, as a witness to the reality of God, so others will be drawn to Him.) As Ruth, I have wondered, "What does my future hold? Will it always be just to struggle through that day and then the next?" Have you felt this way? But, God had a plan for her life that included great blessings, as He does for each of us. Just as Ruth, we, too, will reap joy and blessings as we follow our Lord and obey His leading. Just walk His path, not our own. God was leading her to the "unknown" ahead, growing her faith. You may sense the Lord nudging you to move forward. Yet, you cannot see where that step is taking you. Read on and you will see this on my journey.

Remember, while God knows ALL that is ahead of us, His plan and purpose is that we learn from our journey, grow through our struggles, and become His best, which will always be for our best, too. God simply wants us to trust Him, to know we are safe in His Hand. God gave me the following poem, which reminded me how much God cared for my yesterdays, so how can I not trust Him today and with my tomorrows.

Only God Knows What Lies Ahead

Only God knows what lies ahead
I am to trust, knowing I am safe in His Hand
For he has been molding and shaping me, you see
He has had a purpose for which He has been training me.

The testings, the stretchings have been to strengthen my faith.
He has stayed close to lift me, in times
when I thought I would break.
On just a little further, I can hear my Heavenly Father say,
I love you my child, and it's going to be great.

As I see my life unfolding,
I see His provisions, His care and His grace,
And when He is ready to use me,
His love will shine from my face.

For only God knows what lies ahead
I know that I can trust Him, for my Heavenly Father cares.
More than any earthly father can, you see,
As my Heavenly Father prepares what is best for me.

God gave me just the title on June 25th, 1995. Then, on that third morning, He gave me the rest of the poem. Isn't it interesting that He also gave me the title for this book and its chapters before giving me what I am to write? Normally, we write the body and then find the best title. Do you think that God is showing me that His ways are different than mine? This was not a book to be written by my efforts, but by His leading. Amen?

Now it is time to begin chapter one. I have changed names of those mentioned in this book to respect their privacy. This is not their story, but this book was an assignment my Heavenly Father gave to me, to tell about my journey and His Faithfulness. It was written to encourage those behind me in their journeys and to show you the need to stay focused on the Lord. In the chapters ahead, I will take you through part of my life's journey. As you read about mine, reflect on your own. Think back. What has God been showing you? Have you been listening to Him?

1

~

Dimes or Dollars

Are you wondering why the title "Dimes or Dollars?"

Are you taking the world's dimes, or are you waiting on God's Dollars?

Are you striving for man's success, or are you waiting for God's best?

As you read, my prayer is that you will see those times in your own life when you chose the world's dimes. It may have been a time when you forgot to take your decision or concern to the Lord in prayer asking God to guide you with your choice. Or, you thought God was not answering since it was taking longer than you expected. He must not be listening, so you did it yourself. Maybe you thought it was something that you really didn't need to pray about as you could handle it yourself. We are fairly intelligent, aren't we? That is when we are the most dangerous, and that is when we will choose the world's "dime" every time.

Let me show you the dime and dollar choices I have made. You will read of my struggles and my victories. As I share my journey with you through these chapters ahead, you will see God's care, His grace and His faithfulness.

Going back to the summer of 1985, my husband Jake and I had just moved from Ohio to Orlando, Florida. Almost immediately, I felt at home. I love the tropical look and the warmth year around. Being able to take walks early in the morning or late in the evening with just a lightweight jacket was wonderful! I have always been cold natured and dreaded the winters more each year. So, Florida felt great to me.☺

Soon after moving, I found a church that I loved and knew God had led me there. By the fall of 1987, I was able to join the Bible Study Fellowship class and gained so many wonderful Christian friends during that five-year study. That part of my life was very good!

In Ohio I had been teaching cosmetology to junior and senior high school students in Vo-Tech centers for nine years. The first six years were at a new Vo-Tech School in my hometown. When I moved to another town in Ohio, I took a job at a large city high school and was there for three years until the move to Florida.

Once Jake and I were settled in Orlando, I visited a school close to our home. I thought it would be good to see if I could substitute, but also to find if there were any openings coming up. I learned there were only adults in the program that I was certified to teach. I thought great! No grades or discipline problems! As I was turning in my resume, Lena, my boss-to-be had been reading it over my shoulder. "Ah she said, you have had high school students!" We then had a brief interview to discuss my teaching background. Lena called me a short time later to ask if I would set up the class and teach it with shared-time students from surrounding high schools. The answer was "yes." It was doing what I had enjoyed the previous nine years. I knew "God's timing" was in the surprise offer. God had blessed so much by getting me just the right job at just the right time. The same was also true in this instance. The administration was not sure they wanted to start this new program until I came along. I believe it was only because God's Hand was in it that the timing was right when I walked in.

I was so excited as Lena explained that the program would be set up as a four-hour day; it was perfect! I had worked full time for over twenty years and was looking forward to having a couple of hours a day to do something else for a change! The first year went well. I loved it and the students. At the end of the year, my boss asked if I would be willing to take on another class, which would make me full-time. When I declined, she asked if I would help find the right person. We would need to work well together with the same plan and curriculum, moving both classes together, close to the same level.

After meeting with an applicant three times, I felt sure Carol and I would work well together. Since I wanted to go to Bible Study Fellowship during the day on Wednesdays, I asked

Carol if I took her class on Tuesday, would she take my class on Wednesday. It would give us a chance to get to know the students in the other class, making it easier to blend the classes for special times. Also, if one of us needed to be out for that day, the other could substitute. We both liked the idea so we took it to the administration. The administration gave us the OK two weeks later.

But even with my career and spiritual life going so well, and even though I was living in an area that I loved, my heart was breaking. You see, God wants us to let Him lead in every area of our lives. If we run ahead of Him, going our own way, we will get a "dime" in that area, which will bring much heartache. That is what I had done when it would have been God's plan to give me a dollar.

In looking for that special relationship called "a mate," I ran ahead of God. Oh, yes, I had prayed for the Lord to guide me, but then ignored or reasoned away caution lights when they came on. He was handsome and charming. I felt so good at his side. He said he wanted to go to church and learn God's Word. (Have any of you fallen for that one?)

My heart's desire had been for a godly husband and a marriage where Christ was the center. I also knew that God's answers are always in one of three categories: yes, no, or wait. In looking back, and if I am honest with myself, I knew it then; I was not getting a "yes" from God. I ran ahead and did it my way. My Heavenly Father in love took me to the wood shed for years where He would grow me up, stretch and test my faith. You see, *His plan is not to harm us but to give us hope and a future.* (Jeremiah 29:11) This was a verse God had given to me to hang on to, but not until the fall of 1992. Only after years of praying for my husband and seeing the situation continually worsen, feeling no more hope and my own strength gone, did I feel my Heavenly Father so close that He was carrying me.

A friend of mine in Orlando and her pastor husband had talked with me many times as I struggled through that part of my life. Dee and I had become good friends while going to Bible Study Fellowship for almost four years. She and Craig had become my sounding board, offering wise counsel. When my husband left for Tennessee and soon after that sought a divorce, I asked Craig to show me in God's Word what I was to do. He opened his Bible to 1 Corinthians 7:10-16. He had me read it and then pointed to verse 15 asking me to read it again and saying, "There is your verse." It was as if the words were lifting off the page, as if they were in "3-D." *"But if the unbeliever leaves, let him do so. A believing man or woman is not bound in such circumstances; God has called us to live in peace."* I experienced a cool feeling of relief as the weight was lifted off my shoulders. Then I read verse 16. *"How do you know wife, whether you will save your husband."* For years I had been praying for him, but our situation had continually worsened. Now I believed that God was saying I should let him go. I didn't need to continue struggling in the marriage. I felt released from that burden knowing my Heavenly Father would take care of me, His child. Yes, God would be releasing me, lifting me out of the pain and struggle, but not yet, as I soon discovered.

Right at Christmas time, about two months after my husband had left for Tennessee, I was hearing him say that he no longer wanted the divorce, was willing to work on the marriage and go to Christian counseling with me. I was crying as I hung up the phone after hearing him voice his change of mind because I felt God now telling me to stay with him. Immediately I called the Lanes. When Craig answered, I told him about the call and asked what should I do now? He confirmed what I felt God was saying. Craig said, "I'm sorry; your verse just went out the window." I would not know until later that these friends felt just as I did and grieved over it as I had. They knew in their hearts that my husband really didn't want to stay in the marriage, but he didn't want to lose "material things." We all felt the chance of our making it was slim. The marriage would only work if God were allowed to be a part.

Another Move

The end of May in 1992, I moved to Tennessee, a place where I knew no one except my non-believing husband. This was not easy for me. I had left a place where I had many good Christian friends from my church and Bible Study Fellowship, a place where I had gone through so much spiritual growth. I had left a special job, and the palm trees and warm breezes that I enjoyed. The most difficult was leaving my only son who moved to Orlando a couple of years earlier after graduating from college. It was only nine months since my husband had moved to Tennessee on a job transfer, wanting a divorce. He was angered at my faith in God; but I had moved to be with him to try to save our marriage, because I felt strongly this was what

God was asking.

After moving to Tennessee, I knew this was God's will. I needed to do my part in working on this marriage without compromising my relationship with God, my Father, and Jesus, my Savior. The first six months were very hard and lonely. My husband did not keep any of his promises, one of which was going to a Christian counselor. Another was to go to church with me at least part of the time. Those first six months, it was just "me and the Lord" and that was the way God wanted it. My Lord was the One that I poured out my heart to every day. It was to Him that I looked for comfort, wisdom, strength, guidance and peace that only He can give to His children, even in the midst of a storm.

I told God how lonely I was, having no one to sit down with and share. I wanted someone "with skin on" who could give me the hugs of encouragement that I missed. I lived far from good friends and family members. God gave me a big blessing, though, as I was able to receive two solid hours of good Christian radio Monday through Friday from 8:00-10:00a.m. My neighbors couldn't believe I could get that station, as they couldn't since we lived in a hilly area outside of Knoxville. It was called JOY 62, and that station did give me joy. I knew my Heavenly Father was showing me His love. Often, when I would finish my devotions and quiet time with Him, He would say the same things through His servants on the radio. When we hear the same message from two or three sources, we better take note of it because God is talking. Yes, my Heavenly Father was teaching me that He was all I needed.

I even struggled with finding the church where I felt God

wanted me. I finally found it early in the fall of 1992. For the Bible Study hour I went into a couple's class. A lady invited me to sit next to her, as her husband didn't come to church either. We shared a little and made plans to meet for breakfast one morning. Oh, how I looked forward to that. We enjoyed that visit, and our friendship started. I soon realized Karen had her own set of problems. We would share together, but neither of us had the strength beyond our own problems to help and encourage the other. And so it went into the holidays. Then one of Knoxville's worst winters kept me at home with a lot of quiet time for the Lord and me. As I look back, I can see how much I needed that time to have the faith and strength for what He knew was ahead.

In the spring of 1993 my husband's father passed away. They had not gotten along for years, but I convinced him to go to the funeral for his mother's sake. While he was gone, the Lord gave me another poem. I knew it was for my husband. I didn't know how he would receive it, so I simply laid it on the stand next to his chair and said, "While you were gone, the Lord gave me this poem. I thought you might like to read it." He read it, and never looking up, laid it back down, and focused on the TV. Here is that poem.

"Wasted Years Without Jesus"

Wasted years without Jesus
All is wasted when not lived for him.
All the toil for self and pleasure
Will mean nothing at life's end.

And when you stand before the Lord
On His great judgment day,
What will He say to you
If in this life, you lived it your way.

Wasted years without Jesus
All is wasted when not lived for Him.
All our deeds will be but dust and ashes
Unless we turn from self and sin.

Will you ever desire no longer to waste the years,
To see God's redemptive plan for you?
When we see our need for His forgiveness
We see His love and mercy for us too.

Years would no longer be wasted then,
If on the Lord you are leaning,
For as we go through this life
He's the one who gives life real meaning.

In early spring the women of the church were having a "retreat" at Gatlinburg. That sounded wonderful! Karen and I decided to be roommates in a room for four. This might be a good time to get acquainted with other ladies from the church and have a vacation in scenic Gatlinburg while leaving our problems in Knoxville. We wondered who would share our room. Karen and I were almost ready to go downstairs when our roommates arrived. Ruby and Anne were also friends and had wondered who we would be. I liked them immediately. There was something very special about Ruby. I didn't know it then, but she was to be my special "gift from God." I knew God was doing something as I could feel the joy, but didn't know that God was answering my prayer for the "encourager friend." By the time we were to climb down from our mountain top experience, I knew that I wanted to get to know Ruby better.

When I arrived home, the situation was unchanged but I was keenly aware of a new feeling in me, a feeling of "hope." I never felt that things were hopeless before, for I knew *all things are possible with God.*" However, that had begun to be just head knowledge since moving to Tennessee. I began to feel *"all things"* might be for others, not me. I rejoiced upon learning of God doing something wonderful in the lives of others, but somehow, I couldn't think He would answer my prayers in such a special way. **Have you felt like this? A sense of hopelessness for your situation?**

Sometimes circumstances stretch the faith we have, whether we have caused the problems or not. But remember, I had made the wrong choice in teaming up with an unbeliever. At the time we were dating, I had wanted to believe that my husband simply wasn't mature in his faith; he just needed to be in church and in God's Word to grow, and I could help him. That's what he had SAID he wanted until after we were married. A counselor friend told me; **"If you want to know the truth about who a man really is, watch what he does, not what he says."** There was enough evidence to show me the truth, but I chose to believe a lie, and fell for a world's dime. I

14

also knew that God loved me and was with me in this valley of despair as I had cried out to Him for help. He had given me the blessings of the radio messages and friends. This was the first time since Christmas a year ago that I actually felt hope in my heart. I knew my circumstances were going to change. I had no idea how or even to what degree, but I knew God would work it out for His glory. Before I made that wrong choice, God knew I would choose one of the world's dimes. He also knew my heart; how I loved Him and wanted to serve Him.

While reading God's Word during those days and listening to the radio, my attention was drawn to Peter walking on the water to Jesus. *I realized Jesus was telling me to keep my focus on Him, NOT ON THE CIRCUMSTANCES AROUND ME.* Just as Peter looked down at the water splashing wildly at his feet and was filled with fear, the Lord was showing the same was true with me. I was doing the same. My focus had shifted from Jesus to the circumstances.

Before moving to Knoxville, Kay, a teacher friend in Orlando, had asked me to help her teach a social manners program to 1st through 12th graders. I enjoyed doing this. And, yes, the extra income was needed because within a month, my husband announced he was moving to Tennessee and wasn't going to look back or pay me a dime. I do not know if any of you have ever been, or are in a similar situation, but I hope you know, the only place we can go in a time like this is to the Lord.

I had enjoyed doing this manners business, so upon moving to Tennessee the next spring, I bought that territory and began to set up the program. Normally, certain department stores would host the program, none of which were in Knoxville. I talked with a department store that had been in that area for years who agreed to try it. After I had four sets of classes, I was told that due to remodeling they would not be able to host any classes for a while. Meanwhile, I began holding classes after hours in a few schools and youth centers.

The income at this point was not making much over my expenses, which really upset my husband. When we married, he was in debt without a lot to show for it, so he had moved into my home. When we moved to Florida, I paid off his debts and put the down payment on our house, so we could get a loan. When he left me to move to Tennessee, he thought he would sell our house in Florida, and it should all be his. After all, he had made some payments! That was when I got a lawyer, and my husband learned he wouldn't get everything. In fact, he was going to lose some of the things he had grown accustomed to. It was then he phoned saying he was now ready to work on the marriage. By giving too much over the years I had enabled him big time and was realizing how I was to blame for a lot of what was going on. I was learning how wrong I had been. When we get things out of "God's order" we get into a mess. Takers are never satisfied always wanting more. They also do not appreciate the ones who give. Takers use, and do not respect enablers (the givers), seeing them as being weak. At the same time when the crippling behavior changes, because it had been feeding their selfish nature, they are angry. The Lord has taught me through these painful experiences where I had it all wrong.

By the 1993 Christmas holidays, over 18 months since my move to Tennessee, the stress and tension at home was totally wearing me down. I told my husband I would like to go to

Orlando for a break. He agreed, but he didn't want to go. In fact, he had already lined up some other plans. We agreed to be home New Year's Day.

The visit in Florida was good. Being able to spend time with my son and friends during the Christmas season and to go to First Baptist Church was absolutely wonderful! I also had time to meet with my two counselor friends, who had known about my situation leading into the move to Tennessee. Meeting with each of them over coffee, I shared what was going on at home and that the marriage was not being worked on as my husband had promised. In fact, things were really unraveling. Both listened and said, **"You have had enough."**

Their words were in my thoughts while driving back to Tennessee. They also made me think of Ellen, my counselor friend in Knoxville. We had met a couple of times, and finally she said, "It's not you that I need to talk with. Do you think your husband would come in?" I told her I didn't think so, but she could try. She called and he agreed to meet, but he did not show up. This hadn't surprised me. My mind now focused on the present. Not knowing how things would be when I got home, I just kept on driving and praying. I talked with Jesus almost the whole ten hours of the trip. I asked Him to give me His wisdom and to show me what I was to do.

When I arrived home New Year's Day, 1994, my husband was not home yet. While driving to church the next morning, I was still praying. Then I had a thought that seemed so strong I just knew the Lord was speaking: *"Find Ellen and tell her what is happening."* This would not be easy because of the number of people in each service. I prayed, "Lord, if I see her and she says the same as the counselors in Florida, then I will know that You are asking me to confront my husband with tough love and leave the results in Your Hands." As I sat down with my friends in church, I looked up to the balcony, and there was Ellen. Pushing past my friends, I hurried up the stairs. Seeing me, she asked how things were going. When I told her, Ellen looked at me, squeezed my hand and said **"You have had enough."** I knew that was God's answer. During the service, tears welled up in my eyes, tears not of joy or sadness, but of relief! Then I heard these words from within, *"When only one person works on the marriage, it is never enough. It takes two wanting the marriage and working on it."*

My thirty-minute drive home from church was a time to listen to a favorite tape or just to think. This was one of the times to just think. I thought I would be nervous about facing my husband, if he were home, as confrontation had always been hard for me. In the past couple of years though, I had learned how damaging not confronting is to a relationship. I was surprised at the unusual calm I felt because I was the one who had left the security of a good job. There was no way I could begin to live on what I was making in my new manners business at this point. I also knew from experience that his concern would not be for me. While still living in Florida he had taken everything from my file and desk and hauled it away, hiding it in storage, so that I could not show how much I had contributed financially. What he hadn't known, however, was that a few days earlier I had felt the need to put the important papers in the trunk of my car, so I would have them when my lawyer asked for them. I also remember the feeling of a "sense of urgency" while doing it. So now in Tennessee, oh yes, I knew what I would be facing. Yet, I could sense God's love and protection. My soul was singing and full of joy, though I felt that I was about to walk into the lion's den. When I drove into the driveway, his truck was there. I walked into our home, feeling such a sense of peace, knowing my Heavenly Father was going to take care of me, His daughter.

After greeting my husband, I said, "We need to talk. This is not working. This is not a marriage. It needs to be worked on by both of us. It's time to begin doing those things that were promised nearly two years ago." He refused and said, "If you are not going to get a real job that makes a good income, I don't need or want you and you can just get out." (I just put that statement a lot nicer than he did.)

The next day I contacted a lawyer highly recommended by a Christian lady and went to see him on Wednesday. Later I discovered my husband had gone to a lawyer that same day. When he told the reason for the divorce was because I was a believer, that lawyer refused his case. My husband didn't know that lawyer was also a believer. During the same week that lawyer saw the Christian lady at her place of business and said he had never, in all his years of practice, seen such strong anger against a wife's faith in God. When I called her to thank her for giving me my lawyer's name, she filled me in about the lawyer my husband had tried to hire.

It was now January of 1994. The delay for my husband to get a lawyer worked for my good. My lawyer was able to file first, which ended up protecting me in several ways. I can look back now and see how the Lord was with me every step of the way. Even though God hates divorce, He knew what was in our hearts and minds. I have no doubt of His protection over me during that time.

A New Beginning

The divorce papers were served to my husband in mid January. He found an apartment, but could not move until February, so I allowed him to stay, using the guest bedroom. Those weeks were long and I really appreciated the support of friends. Ruby was checking on me every day, giving me encouragement from God's Word. I knew she was praying for my safety. She told me later that she had never felt comfortable praying for someone to be released from a marriage until mine.

Spiritual Warfare is real, my friends. I remember my lawyer in Florida saying: "There is a fine line between being under conviction and becoming demonically possessed. Be careful." That sent chills down my back. He was the lawyer/counselor I had gone to when my husband was leaving for Tennessee. He took only believers as clients after first trying to put the marriages back together: However, not with ours.

My mind drifted back to the only time my husband had agreed to go to church with me in Tennessee. My lawyer from Florida had warned that he might go to church, even carry his Bible, but that does not mean he is ready to change. If it's not real, he probably wouldn't continue doing that for long. The one time he went in Knoxville was our first Easter there. It was clear he was very uncomfortable. He was in such a hurry to get out of the church after the service, that he pushed me ahead of him down the balcony stairs and out the first exit. A couple of years prior to this, he had a certain bad dream three times. There were a few other happenings that caused him to fear as well. Finally, after he had asked me what I thought about all of this, I simply said, *"Do you think God is trying to tell you something?"* From that point on, my husband became more and more agitated about anything concerning my faith in God.

Later my younger sister told me she feared for my safety. She and her husband had stayed with us several times in Florida. However, the first time they came to stay after we moved to Tennessee, she said she was so relieved when they left. She began crying and told her husband that even though she loved me, she could not stay with us anymore because she felt an evil presence in our home. They didn't tell me that until after my husband had moved out, but they had been praying for me.

It was now the morning after the divorce papers had been served. I was having my quiet time, reading in 2Chronicles 32:1-8. In my devotional, the theme on that section of verses shows us that *with God, we are the majority. As long as we are on the Lord's side, He is with us, fighting our battles for us.* In the application part in my Bible, verse one says, ***"We must take all the steps we possibly can to solve the problem or improve the situation. But also commit the situation to God in prayer, trusting Him for the solution. Trusting Him for the outcome."***

I had just finished my quiet time when the phone rang. It

was my son. The first thing he said was, "Are you all right Mom?" This was not something he normally asked, and I could hear the concern in his voice. He had said I was a "survivor," so he never worried about me, but I knew he was now. I told him what was going on, but that I knew God's protection was with me. I was in God's hands and would be all right. I had so hoped when I had married Jake that he would be the father to my son that his real father had not been, but that was not to be. My counselor friend from church had told me, after hearing my story, that I had been married thirty-one years between these two men and neither should have lasted two years.

I finished the visit with my son and hadn't even gotten up from my chair when the phone rang again. This time it was the Lanes, my friends from Florida, who had been my sounding board. The night before while Craig was reading, he had looked up and told Dee to call me in the morning and ask if I were all right. He said this to her at the same time the divorce papers were being given to my husband. As we visited, Dee shared the concern they had for me. They had asked their church to pray for me for the past three weeks, praying for my release from this marriage. I knew God had put me in their minds to intercede for me. Just as I hung up the phone, it rang again. This time it was my younger sister. Her husband had been reading the paper the night before and put it down to ask her if she had talked with me in the past couple of days. When she said, "no," he said, "Call her in the morning. See if she is all right." Again, he was reading the paper during the exact time the divorce papers were being served. He had felt an urgency to have her call me. He even reminded my sister to call that morning when he left for work. In all three of those calls, the first words spoken to me were **"are you all right?"** As I look back, I realize I was in more danger than I even thought, but I knew that God had His angels watching over me. God is so good to us!

The Lord was also directing me to just the right verses in His Word. Isaiah 40:11 helped me so much before my husband moved out. My devotional summed it up this way. *"Underneath are the everlasting arms. You cannot get below them, so rest in them as a tired child."* That was me! That whole month my husband gave me no money for groceries. He took my name off our accounts; then he bought the groceries, buying only enough for me to fix his dinner, not allowing any leftovers. There was no milk or food for breakfast or lunch since he ate at work. Ruby gave me food from her pantry, which I needed to keep hidden in the truck of my car. I froze milk in small containers for my breakfast because if it were found in the refrigerator, he would pour it down the drain. My older sister and her husband felt led to give her bonus check to me to help me, as they knew the situation. "And my God will meet all your needs." (Philippians 4:19)

It was January 21ˢᵗ; the verbal abuse had worsened. Another Scripture that helped me to feel His protection was Psalm 91: 1,2,11,14 and 15. The theme is God's protection in the midst of danger. From verse 11, *I felt His angels' protecting me,* and in verses 14 and 15 it says, *"because I love Him, He says He will rescue me. He will protect me because I acknowledge His Name. When I call upon Him, He will answer me and will be with me in my trouble. He will deliver me and honor me."*

Does this not show His love for us as absolutely awesome? At this point, I had no more strength and knew He was carrying me. **His tired child was resting in His arms.**

The time finally came when my husband moved into his apartment. What a relief! I filled my time at home with being in God's Word, listening to gospel music while praising and thanking Him for the answers to prayer, even beyond what I was praying for. (Ephesians 3:20) I knew others were bathing me with prayers and that is such a blessing. As I open my journal to that time, I note more friends and family were calling to check on me, to encourage and to pray with me, than at any other time. I received more cards and letters than usual. The best part was knowing that my Heavenly Father was laying me on their hearts and minds to intercede for me.

Since my husband was now out of the house, my younger sister came to stay for a week in mid February because she and her husband were concerned about me. We had such a good time: shopping, eating out, walking and talking. My sister was surprised at how well I was doing. It was because God had just begun to release me from a painful situation. The joy of thankfulness in my heart to Him was overflowing.

The divorce date was set for April 29th. My lawyer was amazed it was set so soon. He was also relieved after meeting my husband during the deposition that was ordered. He, too, had seen Jake's anger about my faith. During this time I could feel God's nearness. Every day, my devotions and the Scriptures were so special. It seemed they had been penned just for me and that time in my life. I knew He was speaking to me each morning. Now that my husband had left, I could feel

God's peace in my home and the joy of His presence with me.

One of the prayers the Lord answered in such a special way was in the selling of the house. My husband wanted to get a realtor and have me removed from the house as soon as possible. If he couldn't be there, he didn't want me there either. I asked my lawyer if I could put a sign in the yard to sell it myself. He said, "Go for it." It would take time for my husband to get any orders from the judge, but if I were actively working at it, the judge would give me the time.

Within the first two weeks of having the "for sale" sign in the yard and with no other advertisement, I had a nibble. The next week, another couple "just happened to drive by." Our home wasn't in an area that was easy for a newcomer to find. They had looked at over forty homes in the Knoxville area already, being disappointed with everything they had seen. As they drove by, they loved the outside of our house, so they came to the door. I happened to be home and so I was able to show it to them. They adored it. They were measuring and placing furniture before they left.☺ They also agreed to let me stay in the home until my classes were completed in mid May. He had sold some homes himself, so he knew how to write the contract and would go with the dates I needed to protect me. It was a big "Thank you Lord" day! God had sold the house in only three weeks!

Something similar had happened when I sold the house in Florida, as God's Hand was in that as well. What are the odds on this happening again? I didn't need to know the odds, as I knew my Lord and Savior was taking care of me. There are no "happenings" that the Lord wasn't working out. He was the one who led that couple right to my door at just the right time. When the divorce was postponed one week, the new owners had quickly agreed to move the date on the closing out another week as my lawyer felt that would work out better if it were after the divorce.

The day for the divorce had been moved from April 29th to May 6th. My verse for that day was Romans 8:28. ***"And we know that in all things God works for the good of those who love Him, who have been called according to His Purpose."*** In looking back, God's timing was perfect. I didn't even realize "how perfect" until I reread my journal recently. At that time, I knew I would need a storage unit until I knew where I was to go. But I didn't know what size because I did not know what the judge was going to award me. The only storage in the small town where I lived was close to the house, but they had no units to rent. On May 4th, a unit opened up, and it was just the right size, as God knew my need.☺

I also felt strongly that the Lord had shown me I was to get away for a couple of months for rest, protection, and have time with Him, praying and asking Him where He wanted me to go, and what I was to do now. My next classes in the business would not be until the fall. The door had opened for me to stay in a small efficiency apartment in Orlando. Some friends from church were going to loan me enough to furnish it, so I could drive down without worrying about a move. That, my friends, was just a couple of the many ways that my Heavenly Father showed His care over me during that time.

The closing on the house was set for Monday, May 9th. On Friday, May 6th, my husband and his lawyer tried to delay the divorce again as they wanted the closing prior to the divorce. My lawyer was very concerned about that, but I felt at peace, as I knew that God was in control. The judge denied the delay stating this divorce would go on as scheduled. It was a long day; my husband tried so hard to prove false things, and even tried to take certain accounts that were mine before we had married. Finally, the judge said that He had made it a habit not to reach decisions when he was tired, so he said we would meet next week on Tuesday morning, May 10th to hear his decision about our assets. Then he looked at me and smiled while saying, "But this divorce is granted on this day."

On Monday, Ruby came over in the morning to help me pack and Mary, a friend from church, came that afternoon. The closing on the house was set for 4:00. My ex-husband was upset when he found out the new owners were letting me stay until I finished the classes that Saturday. He had wanted things to be as difficult for me as possible, but I knew my Lord was blocking all of those things he was trying to use to hurt me.

I also felt God was doing something else special here. In January, the nation-wide chain of department stores that hosted most of the programs like I was teaching had just bought out two stores in Knoxville malls. When I had met with them, we had set up the two programs that I was just finishing. We also "tentatively" set up two more in the fall to begin right after Labor Day. This was why I needed to stay in the house until after the programs were completed. I wanted to stay focused on doing a good job for future business if this was to be God's way of providing for me. My ex-husband had the security of his job. I was starting over with a new business, which at this point

27

would not be able to support me.

Tuesday, May 10th came. I was up even earlier than usual, as I was anxious to see what God would reveal to me from His Word. The scripture was Psalm 18:1-19. As I read, tears of joy were streaming down my face. The theme for this Psalm is: **Gratitude for deliverance and victory.** *Verse 6 "From His temple He heard my voice; my cry came before Him, into His ears." Verses 16-19 "He reached down and drew me out of my trials. He rescued me from my powerful enemy, from my foes, who were too strong for me. He brought me out into a spacious place; He rescued me because He delighted in me."* As I sobbed, all I could say was **"Thank you Jesus, thank you for rescuing me."** I was so weary of this battle and had no strength left. He had rescued and carried me through it. I knew the divorce was over now; it was up to the judge what assets would be mine.

My lawyer already told me there was no way I would be able to recoup all the monies I had put into this marriage. But, I knew the spiritual growth I had gained in these years was worth it all. And, God had given me many precious friends on this journey. They are His precious jewels; more valuable than anything I had lost. The money was all His to begin with anyway. I did have many friends praying for the judge to show God's mercy on me. I also knew that the Lord could guide the mind of the judge as He did the kings of nations, so I was in God's hands no matter what happened. I did add a special prayer of my own that I will be sharing with you.

As the judge came into his chambers he looked at me and smiled. Then he looked at my ex-husband, squinted his eyes and pinched his lips together and said, "In reviewing this case, it was clear this never was a marriage from day one." **That was what my special prayer had been;** that the judge would see that truth and say that to my ex-husband. The judge then turned to me and started listing the things that were mine to keep. Since the closing on the house was after the divorce, but before the judge's decision, the monies had been put in holding just the day before. The judge gave back to me, off the top, the monies I had put down on the house in Florida and part of the monies I had used to pay off my ex-husbands debts, as it was from a trust I had before the marriage. We were to split what was left.

I have shared this part of my journey for you to see not only what happened when I ran ahead of God and chose my dime, but to see my Lord's care and His grace in my life have been overwhelming. I have been so undeserving of such a love as His. Do you feel the same way? How can we ever really understand the depths of God's love and grace for us? We fall so short of being what we should be for Him. So often we fail to pray for or wait on His Dollars. As this book continues, you will see not only the choices that relate to the title of each chapter, but also what else was going on in my life and how I felt at that time to show you the whole picture of my journey. I pray that each of you reading these chapters will see His love, His power, and His grace when we do give Him first place in our hearts and lives.

Going back to this past February 22nd, after my ex had moved out, Ruby had called to say our friend, Anne, the 4th roommate at the ladies retreat, was leaving for Mayo Clinic that afternoon for a surgery she had only a small chance of surviving, but none without it. I wanted to do or give her something to encourage her before she left. I prayed and asked God to give me a poem for her, and He did! She survived that surgery, and several more in the following years before the Lord took her home. She had kept my hand written poem in the front of her Bible, reading it often, as that was God's gift to her through me. As I reread the last lines, I knew it was for me as well. He had been telling me the whole month between January 21st and February 22nd, I was to rest in His Arms. This is the poem God gave me to bless both of us ladies, and maybe it will bless some of you, too.

Sometimes He uses our testimony
Of joys and peace and gain,
Other times He uses sickness,
Sorrow, death and pain.

For it is with His all-knowing wisdom,
He guides us while holding our hand
For He sees the path before us
And how we are to fit into His plan.

So lean back in His Everlasting Arms
And let Him carry you through,
For however He uses us for His glory
Will be for our very best, too.

2

Just "a Dime" (the world)

Once upon a time, a man was at his nephew's house.
He said, "Johnny, would you like a dime today or a dollar
tomorrow?" Little Johnny thought. The dime would buy
a bag of potato chips that he liked so much, but he also
wanted a rubber ball and that would take the dollar. He
thought some more; he was hungry now so he decided to
take the dime. So, his uncle gave him his dime and little
Johnny ran to the corner store and bought the potato
chips. He opened the bag. They smelled so good, that he
ate and ate the whole bag of chips. Next morning little
Johnny's friends were playing outside with their rubber
balls; so he ran to his uncle's house and rang the
doorbell. When his uncle opened the door, he was
surprised to see Johnny and asked what had brought him.

Little Johnny said with excitement he had come to get his dollar to buy the rubber ball he had been wanting. His uncle said, "But, Johnny, yesterday I asked you if you wanted a dime then or a dollar today. You decided to take the dime then, so there is no dollar today."

I heard this story in the fall of 1992 on the Joy 62 radio station that God had blessed me with during those first two years in Tennessee. This was during the time the Lord wanted me to learn to lean on Him alone. When I heard this story, I sobbed and sobbed, as I knew God was teaching me an important lesson. Learning to wait on God and His timing and not to run ahead of Him. I had reasoned away the warning signs. I wanted the potato chips today. I did not want to think about how wrong that decision was, nor that it was not God's choice for me. I wanted this good-looking, charming man as my husband. Together, he would learn how to grow in the Lord, and we would have this wonderful Christian marriage: Satan's lies. Satan is good at taking Gods truth and twisting it so that we will not see his lie. I believed I could save this man from himself, helping him to become what God wanted him to be. Looking back at my reasoning, I'm appalled. Who did I think I was? I would not be able to do any such thing unless God chose to use me as His vessel. It's not us, but the Lord who draws others to Him.

We all must have valleys in our lives, as this is where God strengthens our faith in Him as He teaches us His lessons we have yet to learn.

The valley isn't our destination.
We must go through the valley to reach "His Purpose."
How long we stay in the valley,
Is sometimes up to us.... Because our doubt and
disobedience cause detours.

In this chapter, we are going to look at some dimes, or choices that are simply made in our own understanding or desires without asking God for His leading. Some of our wrong choices have bigger or longer consequence than others. My choosing a mate without God's blessing caused years and years of pain and discouragement, and this could have lasted for the rest of my life on earth.

With the divorce behind me, I was on my own with very little income. I look back to where I was before I made that wrong choice of marrying a world's dime. I had a nice little home nearly paid for. My furniture and car were debt free. I loved my career, my church and was still living in my hometown with family and friends close by. My life was peaceful, but I was lonely. I loved my Lord and Savior and was growing some in my spiritual life, but often we do not grow deep in our faith until we are in the valley of despair. I struggled with backsliding before I could get close and rooted deep in the Lord.

After I married my ex, I had stopped going to church, because he would not go with me. Soon the daily devotions were not getting done. My prayer life dwindled to a few quick prayers as I felt God was so far away. He was, but guess who moved. I had! There is no such thing as sitting on the fence with God. One day I woke up and realized I had strayed from God. Shocked, I ran after Jesus and hung on to Him "white knuckled" while pleading for His help to get back to His path.

At that point, my burning desire was to become an instrument God could use to draw others to Him. No longer could I waste this life He had given me. Then I understood the need for total surrender to my Lord and Savior. I had made a mess with my choice. But as a small child gives her mother a tangled bunch of yarn to straighten out, I gave the mess in my life to Jesus and asked Him to straighten it out in a way that would glorify Him. That is what He waits for us to do. It has been a painful process, but just as a good father will discipline his child to help him become his best, our Heavenly Father does the same with us.

With my divorce a new season of my life was unfolding. It was time for me to move forward into the unknown for me, but with my best friend, my Lord and Savior leading the way. My Heavenly Father knew I was exhausted and needed a time to be with Him, to look for His answers. Friends moved my things into storage. Then my lawyer told me I could not leave town until some papers were processed that I must sign. The lady, who had given me my lawyer's name, discovered I needed a place for a few days. She invited me along with my eighty-five (85) pound dog to stay at their home. Now my dog Suzie was a sweetheart and everyone loved her, but that was really going the extra mile. They felt I should be safe there, as my ex didn't know them or where they lived. This young lady said she knew I loved the Lord. They had an extra bedroom and felt this was what God wanted them to do. Wow! What more can I say.

When God asks us to do something to help our fellow believers and we obey, He will bless.

Before leaving for Florida, I talked with Ellen, my counselor friend from my church in Knoxville. She questioned why I was leaving, knowing that I had set up two more classes to be started in the fall with the department store. One class was scheduled in each of their stores right after Labor Day. After we talked, she agreed I did need some rest and time for God to show me where He wanted me and what I was to do. It would also give my ex time to cool down, so I would be safer. I told her a local dentist was willing to hire and train me as a dental assistant in his office. In Tennessee, I could be trained on the job, along with some night school to be licensed in that state. I felt this would give some regular income along with the manners classes. Ellen thought it sounded like a heavy schedule; but said when I was ready to come back, not to worry about a place to stay. They had a basement apartment in their home for missionaries, but it would be mine until I could get on my feet. Wow!! More of God's blessings!!

I gave Ellen an approximate return date. I would need to be back to do the advertisement and then the registration for the classes. While in Florida, I would be checking on an opening at the school where I had taught cosmetology before, along with seeing what it would take to become licensed in Florida as a dental assistant. I also added, I was praying for God to open or close doors, to direct me where He wanted me, and into the job that He was going to use for my provisions. With that, she gave me a hug and said she would be praying for me. Isn't God good? He had provided the precious couple who had given the safe shelter when I needed it before leaving, a small apartment was ready for me in Florida, and now, a place to stay if I felt God was directing me back to Knoxville. God's grace is beyond my understanding. In a short time, God had blessed me with not one, but three temporary homes. I should not worry as He was taking care of His child, because He loves me and I had cried out for His help and mercy. The main key for His abundant love was the fact that I had given Him the control over my life and simply wanted to rest in His Everlasting Arms. All I could say then, and now, is "Thank you, Jesus."

Two days later with my car packed and my dog, Suzie, taking the whole back seat, we were on our way.☺ Now is a good time to tell you how I acquired Suzie.

Suzie is one of God's very precious gifts. She was always there for me, loving me in her special way, and could really read my emotions. In early September of 1990 while still in Orlando, someone had dumped this little puppy at the school where I taught. She followed my students to our classroom as the girls had fussed over her. They burst in the door, calling for me to look at this puppy as she curled up at the door, shaking. She was starving and had a bad case of fleas. I walked to the cafeteria with a couple of the girls to find some food. It was between breakfast and lunch, so soft ice cream was the only choice. When we got back, one of girls was feeding her animal cookies. I laughed saying, "We're feeding cookies and ice cream to a starving puppy!" I put her into a box cushioned with the lab towels, and she slept through class time. I took her to the vet and was told this puppy had gone about as far as she could go when she had reached my classroom door; between

36

starving and the fleas, she would not have lasted much longer. The vet kept her a few days to make sure she would be all right. None of the girls' parents would agree to take her. I already had a poodle and didn't want another dog, but she was so cute. I told the vet I would take care of her until I could find a good home.

I was telling a friend about this puppy I didn't know what to do with. She laughed, *"Don't you know God is trying to give this dog to you?* For some reason, that only God knows, you are supposed to keep her." Well, I knew this dog had won my heart. The vet thought she would be about 35-40 lbs. full-grown. However, the golden retriever and collie in her showed up causing her to grow to a beautiful 85 pounds. Ha! For the next 6 1/2 years, she was to be my buddy. I had named her Suzie, after calling her Suzie-Q at first. She has been the sweetest dog I've ever had.

Wow! We made it. Almost fourteen hours since leaving Knoxville, due to stops for Suzie's walks.

Soon after getting my little apartment set up, one of my dearest friends from Bible Study Fellowship days took me to their cottage in Boca Grand, Florida. It was a great get-away time to laugh, cry, and share together. Suzie enjoyed the walks and the ocean breezes, too. It was the relaxing time that my friend Gayle (and my Lord) knew I needed.

While in Orlando I attended a divorce recovery class at my church. During that time, I dated one man from the class who had been divorced for years. But even though we had enjoyed our time together, I realized this was not God's choice for me. I would need more healing before I was to even think about going there again. I also knew I needed to get on my feet financially. My Heavenly Father had rescued me, and I was in His care. As my encourager friend from Knoxville would say to me, *He hasn't brought you this far to let you down.*

The two months flew by. The jobs and schooling I checked out were "closed doors." Remember, I had prayed for Jesus to show me clearly open or closed doors. How much I had wanted to move back to Orlando. But, even more I wanted to be where God wanted me. All signs kept pointing me back to Knoxville.

The time had come to say that tearful good-bye to my son and friends again. I headed back to Knoxville to see if the manners class or the dental assistant job, or the combination of the two was the Lord's leading. Ellen said the apartment was waiting and so was she. Knowing that I would be staying with my good friend and counselor gave me more peace going back.

A little over fourteen hours later, I pulled into Ellen's drive. She came out to greet me, but when she saw Suzie, she had a surprised look on her face. She said, "I forgot about your dog! My husband doesn't know about her!" My stomach did a flip-flop as I thought, where would I go now if I can't stay here? He agreed to Suzie staying with me, but I was to keep her on the tile and not let her on the carpet. The apartment faced out to their pool and was absolutely gorgeous. Less than two weeks later I came home to find their whole family watching their daughter's wedding video on the TV in my living room. Guess who was on a beanbag chair on the carpeted area with their new son-in-law? You guessed it! Suzie had made a hit with them as they were laughing while saying she was part of the family. She had sat on that chair with each of them and was thoroughly enjoying the attention. I was even told that when I got into the pool, she could also go in. She had won their hearts. ☺

That first couple of weeks back in Knoxville, I hit the ground running. First I found an apartment in a nice area, with a large grassy area to walk Suzie. But I had to wait for a vacancy. Then I made contact with the stores to assure the classes were still set for the week following Labor Day. They were; so the next step was getting a phone number for my ads. I called the phone company to see how we could do this, as I did not yet have an address or place for a phone hook up. The lady was very nice as I explained that I needed the number for the advertisements, but was staying with friends until my apartment was available. She said I could get a "surrogate voice mail." Then I could retrieve the messages from any phone and return the calls. I contacted the printer to start working on the business paperwork since a phone number was now available to be placed on them.

I told Ellen about getting the phone number and how it would work. I also told her that Mary, a friend from church, had offered the use of her condo during the day to return calls. However, I would also need a phone during the evening hours; I hadn't figured that one out yet. Later that day, Ellen told me she had talked with her husband and he had suggested I use a phone on their third floor. It was on a separate line. Since Suzie would be just steps away, I could even take breaks to walk her. What a blessing!

I was now able to catch my breath a little bit. My friends were amazed as one hurdle after another was taken care of. I was able to take a little more time for a breakfast, lunch or dinner with friends. Ruby, my encourager, shared breakfast time with me once or twice a week as we thanked God together for His care. She was also the one who had given me the name of the dentist who said that he would hire and train me as one of their dental assistants. It was time to contact him to see how we would work out the timing, if that were still what God had for me.

It had been three weeks since my arrival back in Knoxville. I talked with the dentist the end of that week. He said they weren't ready yet as the new addition had gone slower than planned. But, yes, he still wanted me to work for him. Actually, I was relieved. It would be easier if the next two programs at the department stores were finished before I began my training.

The big day was here. It was Sunday, three weeks before classes were to begin, the day when the stores' advertisement for those classes would be in the paper. I had no idea how well the response would be. I only knew that is how we get most, if not all of the students who attend these classes. Would I have enough students to pay my upcoming apartment rent along with my other bills? I was also a little nervous that none would be able to reach me yet by phone, only to hear my voice mail. Would they give up and not leave a message? I knew that I was not to worry about any of this as **I had done all that I could. God wanted me to trust Him to take care of the outcome.**

As I was leaving for church that morning, Ellen was going out to their car to go to church also. She asked how I felt. I smiled while saying, "I've done all I can; it's in God's hands now. We'll see if this is what God has for me to do." She smiled reassuringly and gave me a hug. As soon as church was over, I needed to get home to man the phone, as my voice mail only held 21 messages.

After changing my clothes and taking Suzie for a quick walk, I headed up to the third floor to see if I had messages to retrieve. There were twenty-one messages, so I began to return calls as quickly as possible. As fast as I was retrieving the calls, more calls were coming in. I gave them my mailing address for them to register their daughters. It was late in the afternoon before I got the calls waiting on my voice mail below seventeen. By that time I needed a break! As I rounded the corner for the last flight of stairs, Suzie was lying at the bottom of the landing waiting for me. Her loyalty was amazing!☺ To make a long story short and get straight to the praise report, I ended up with 91 students at one stores and 107 at the other!! Wow! (Normally, good numbers across the country were about 30.) Isn't God good!

Survival Begins

The classes began the week following Labor Day. It was an extremely busy time as my apartment had become available and moving day was the day before the first class was to begin. Also, Anne Graham-Lotts, (Billy Graham's daughter) was holding a three-day ladies conference. I managed to squeeze in part of the classes as I was stepping over bags and boxes while trying to get ready for the first class. As Suzie watched, I think she sensed that this might be a lonely evening for her. I stopped to pet and love on her while thinking; maybe it would have been better to have waited and moved the first of the week.

When I told Ellen an apartment was ready, she asked, "What was the hurry?" I felt it was time to get on my feet. I didn't like taking help; I had always been a giver. But, this was a lesson the Lord was teaching me. ***If we can't take help when we're down, we have pride that needs to go.*** Other believers had been blessing me with their help now for the past several months, and I knew God was providing for me through these precious friends, but it was still hard for me. It feels much better to give than to receive, but there are times when God says it is time for us to allow others the blessing of giving. When we are able to help others, it is a good feeling knowing we are able to bless them; but if they resist our help, it takes away the joy of giving. Is this what I was doing to Ellen? I assured her that without her help, I don't know what I would have done. But when the apartment became available, it was time to step out in faith, trusting in my Heavenly Father's provisions.

The classes were going well and Suzie and I were getting used to our new home. The National Director from whom I had purchased the territory to do the manners classes called and asked if I would like to buy the whole state of North Carolina and develop it for the price of one territory. I prayed about it as I thought, "How can I do all of this and work for the dentist as well?" As I was praying, something kept popping into my mind that one of the pastors in my church in Florida had said; *"If you aren't sure what God is wanting you to do and you are praying about it, keep moving until you bump into a door, (but don't try* to climb over it). *You can't know if there is a closed or open door if you are standing still. If you come to a door, God will direct you where to go from there. If there is no door, keep moving."*

The department store chain that hosted my program was also in North Carolina. I contacted their regional office; they faxed me the areas of store locations, phone numbers, and the store managers' names. I made calls to the department stores in North Carolina. Things moved along quickly and before I had completed the two sets of classes in Knoxville, I had two more programs set up in North Carolina. One of the programs was to run in Charlotte, then one in Ashville. Both wanted to start after the holidays, so the registration would need to be completed before the holidays. I checked with the dentist to see if he knew when he would need me to start. The office addition was still moving slowly and until it was completed, there was no need to expand with more employees. He rescheduled a day for me to come in to observe. He also asked if I would be willing to be trained to do a special treatment on children's teeth to whiten them. That would be a step higher in training and pay, which sounded good to me.

The graduation of both sets of classes in Knoxville was completed now. Parents were already calling to enroll their daughters in the spring sessions. Thank you, LORD!! Only God could have given me these numbers. The parents, students and department stores were all elated with the program.

The week following the end of those two fall sessions was my observation day with the dentist. One of the procedures was a tooth being filled on an eight-year-old girl who had just finished my classes. She was so scared, but I was able to talk with her and get her mind off the procedure, making the dentist's work easier. Her mother was also telling me how much they had enjoyed the classes. Steve, the dentist, told me later that he was impressed with how I was able to calm the girl down by just talking with her. After hearing her mother rave about my program, he was also impressed with it!

I thought back over my day when I got home for the evening as Suzie and I went for our walk. I talked to her awhile, and then I talked with my Lord. How had my day gone? I had enjoyed some of the things at Steve's office, and he seemed very easy to work with, but I wasn't sure this was God's plan. Why did I feel a hesitation in my spirit? "Lord," I said, "I know You opened the door at this dental office for the timing has been so good. Right down to the delay. It would be a steady income while the social manners program was not guaranteed. The few little classes I had done last winter were not enough income to buy groceries. The first two classes last spring after the department store had opened, which were normal sized classes, would have paid my bills, but without any extra for the slower summer months ahead.

My finances had improved since the fall programs. I was excited as I could feel and see God's Hand in my new business. The class numbers and program acceptance both had been overwhelming. But I also knew, at this time, I could do only two sets of classes a year at each of the two stores, one set in the fall, one in the spring. The earnings from the two fall sessions were enough to pay my bills through January. Next question, how well will it go in North Carolina? If it does, I will need helpers. I had used a couple of ladies this round, just to help with the graduation and the grand finale fashion show. But if North Carolina went well, I would need some ladies who would be reliable and able to teach some of the classes. My mind was spinning. "Lord, I need direction from you… clear direction, so that I don't take any detours, and also so I don't miss what You have for me. The steady income from being a dental assistant, which was a field where there was a demand, meant job security. For us ladies, that's a biggy, but You know that Lord since You created us women. But, what is it that You are leading me to do? I want what You want for me, Lord. I want to follow Your plan, knowing Your plan will not only be for my best, but for Your glory."

The registration was about to begin for the first class in Charlotte, North Carolina. The ad would be in their newspaper the following Sunday. I had gotten an 800 number for them to reach me. I continued to pray, **"Lord, I need to hear Your voice, to see Your hand in this."** As registration for Charlotte began, I also needed to know if becoming a dental assistant was in God's plan. The dentist would need to know soon if he were to hire someone else. He was a fellow believer and I wanted to be fair with him, so I prayed a special prayer. I prayed for a certain number of student enrollments in my mailbox that next day to show me I was not to worry about needing another income, and I was not to divide my time between the two. If the number was not there, then the door was still open to becoming a dental assistant. I don't pray that way often, and when I do, I don't pray for gain, but for an answer. God knows our hearts and will know the difference.

The next afternoon, I went to my mailbox to see what the registration numbers were. Sitting in my car with the envelopes on my lap, I first prayed, "Lord, I pray that Your answer is here, right in front of me." I nervously counted the envelopes. A wave of disappointment went through me, as the number of envelopes was quite a few less registrations than I had prayed for. In my spirit I said, "OK, Lord, I can work both jobs if that is Your plan, but only with Your help." In my mind, I knew it would be very difficult. I would have little time for anything or anyone else. I took a deep breath and began to open the envelopes. The first one was a double, then a triple, then another double, then four cousins, and on and on the numbers climbed to, you guessed it, the exact number that I had asked the Lord to give me. I had not thought of my prayer being answered this way. Not one over, nor one under, but exactly. *I believe our Heavenly Father smiles with joy as He surprises us with His answers in ways that stretch our faith, while showing us He is in perfect control.* I was in the business over six more years and never again did I get so many duplicates in one day, not even in an entire program! The Lord couldn't have spoken any clearer. I sat there with goose bumps all over me and with tears running down my cheeks. I knew my Lord and Savior had just revealed a small amount of His Power, which looked "huge" to me. He had also shown me His mighty love and care. *I have learned never to underestimate Him, or to give up too quickly, as He is never late!*

As I burst through the door of my apartment, I gave Suzie a big hug. She didn't know why I was so excited, but she knew I was, so was excited with me.☺ I had picked up some chicken at

KFC on the way home, which she liked added to her dinner. After a hearty meal, we took our usual evening walk. The air was getting cooler now as we were nearing the end of October, but it felt good. My mind was spinning again with all that had taken place since the divorce in early May. God had blessed me so many times since then. Yet, there was still fear in me. What if this doesn't work? I mean, I'm fifty years old now. I don't have too much time left to start over.

Soon Suzie and I were back home from our walk. While taking her leash off as I opened the door, I turned and looked at my Honda in the parking lot; a tinge of fear swept over me. It had been a good car, but it was seven years old. Some friends had been voicing their concerns about the miles I would be driving to develop the North Carolina territory. They thought I was expecting a lot out of my little blue Honda that had reached just over 200,000 miles. Then as I walked through the door, I remembered the excitement I had felt earlier because of God's latest miracle with the exact number of registrations for me. Oh, how soon we let Satan rob our joy by allowing him to whisper in our ear, planting seeds of fear, worry, or whatever he knows will get our attention off God and on the situation or ourselves. I immediately told the Lord that I was sorry, for I know when I fear the "what if's" or worry, I'm not trusting Him, and knowing that He can and will take care of me. He said I was to trust Him! It sounds so simple. But I find that it is a lesson I must learn over and over, every day and every moment.

I called Steve, the dentist, the next morning and said that we needed to talk. He suggested we have lunch together. I told

Steve about my prayer, my concern over how I could do both jobs, but also about my fear of not having a good job with a dependable income. Then I told him God's answer that came in the mail. With that, Steve looked at me and said, "Who am I to argue with God? It is clear that He is leading you to do the manners programs. He has opened up North Carolina and He is going to take care of you. Yes, I was looking forward to your becoming part of our office. You would have fit in well, but I will find someone else. It will work out just fine." He gave me one of his big smiles while saying, "God's in charge, remember? But if ever down the road you need or want this job, it will be here." I was so relieved to get that taken care of and know Steve was in agreement. It was another confirmation God was leading me to do just the manners program.

When Ruby heard how God had answered my prayer in such a special way, she was so excited. Then I told her about my visiting Steve. She asked why I thought God had opened this dental assisting job so easily? I gave a big sigh as I spoke slowly for the words were expressing my innermost feelings that I had not thought through yet, only felt. I said I felt God had opened the door to the possibility of that job (or career) because at that time, *my hope and faith were shaken. I needed a sense of security.* God in His grace had given me that with the first and only dentist I had approached about a job. In looking back at the ways my Lord and Savior was showing me His care over these past few months, I knew He was stretching me to take a new step of faith; one that shows I trust Him with my future. For me to have the courage not to choose the world's way of security with a steady income was extremely hard, yet that was what the Lord was asking me to do. But when I look back at His care, how could I not see that the only security is with Him. How can I not trust Him? If I reasoned with the world's mindset, I would have taken the "world's dime" for the wrong reason, the security it offered. There was nothing wrong with Steve or this job. I had prayed for an answer from God, and He had given me His answer. *Take this step with Me, trust Me for your provisions, watch for the testimony I will give you through My blessings.* At that point, Ruby said, **"I believe God wants you to share your story some day with other ladies to help them see God's grace and His care are for all who will trust Him."**

One of the prayers God answered at this time was upgrading my 1987 Honda to a 1992. I had been praying about all of the driving I was facing in developing the North Carolina territories. I didn't feel paying for a new car made good financial sense, so I prayed for a two-year-old white Honda in excellent shape with blue interior and blue pinstripes. I looked at a couple of lots but nothing felt right. At one close to my home I saw a pretty gold-colored 1994 with a sunroof, which really caught my eye. The salesman told me the price, more than I felt comfortable with, so I told him what I was looking for. He pointed two rows back. There it was! Just what I had prayed for: white with blue interior and pinstripes. I chose the one I knew was God's answer. It had been well taken care of with only a few more miles than the gold one. It turned out to be a great car that I drove for seven more years! The only thing I wasn't sure I liked at first was that it was four-door. But God knew that was what I would need for the business, so He threw that one in.☺ And, I did need the four doors! Again, I could have chosen the world's dime, the one that would have given me a higher debt, had not been taken care of as well, and had only "two doors." But I took the one God had for me, the one He had blessed for me.

During this same time, there was another area in my life that I need to share with you before this chapter can be completed. God's Hand again guided me to a victory in making a right choice. It is about a relationship that had started to form with a very nice man. He had been instrumental in helping me to set up the business paperwork for teaching this program since I had started it two years before. We had a good business relationship, and I had only thought of him in that way. I had given him devotionals I enjoyed reading, since he didn't currently go to church, and he seemed to appreciate them. He did not know anything about my personal life until the divorce was almost completed. I told him I was going to Florida for a couple of months and I may stay there. If I came back, my phone number and address would be different since I would move to Knoxville. I needed to know how much extra time he would need to make the changes on the store signs and flyers. That way I would know how soon I needed to have things in place to be able to do the fall classes that were set up. When I came back, naturally I called him to get the paperwork started for the fall programs.

After the programs had begun, he asked me if I wanted to go out for dinner and then play miniature golf. After we had gone out a few times, I found I was enjoying our times together, but I only thought of him as a friend. He had not dated for a

few years, pouring himself into his business. I was encouraged
by his interest in reading the devotional, which we discussed a
lot. We continued to see each other as friends, neither of us
having much time with our businesses, but we would work in a
movie here, or a game of tennis there.

As the holidays rolled around, it was clear he wanted to be
more than just friends. I had to tell him that I would not be
interested in a more serious relationship with anyone who didn't
have God as an important part of his life. He said he had
wanted to go to church. As I talked about my church life a lot,
he was hoping I would ask him to go with me. After listening
to me, (I am usually pretty vocal about my faith and my Lord)☺
and reading the devotionals, he wanted to go to a good church
but didn't know where to go. Also, he had not wanted to go
alone.

Now, I have been extremely careful in that area, having
been fooled before. We always need to learn from our mistakes,
so we do not repeat them. I remember Charles Stanley saying
one time; *"If you don't learn the lesson God intends for you to,
He will put you back on the wheel of life and spin it again.
Now, it's up to us how many times we want to spin."* Not only
did I NOT want to spin on the wheel of life again, but I also did
not want to waste the time left in my life. God wants us to live
our lives His way, not ours. While I wanted to see my friend
enjoy a personal relationship with Jesus, I also knew I needed to
be careful about my "savior mentality."

I told him he could go with me the first time to see if he
liked the church, but if he wanted to continue, he would need to
go on his own. I wanted him to go to church for himself and

not for me. I told him I knew it isn't easy going to church alone. He continued coming to church for the next month or so. He did begin a Bible study class and seemed to be enjoying it as we talked about what he was learning. In my heart, I knew as long as he looked to me, I needed to question his motive. Then, as I was praying about it, I knew God was saying *"Cut him loose. See if he's only doing this for you or if it's important to him for himself. If it is, he will continue the classes and church for himself."*

Confronting someone with something that may be painful is something I have always struggled with. I have had to learn that most of the time it is for the best. But, it is still hard for me. God knows that. So the next day as I was listening to Chuck Swindoll on the radio, he said something that I needed to hear. ***"You can be as unequally yoked if you are a mature believer and marry a new or baby believer as you would be if you married a non-believer. You are still at totally different levels of faith and understanding."*** As I listened to the rest of his message, I realized how right that was. Even though I had not given any serious thought to marriage at this point, I realized there were a couple of times I had entertained the thought of "what if." But as my focus had remained on Jesus and what He had ahead for me, I could see that my friend could not be the one for me, as his spiritual walk had not yet begun. And what had I prayed for? If my heart's desire for that special mate were ever to be in God's plan for me, that prayer would be answered with a man of His choosing. That man would also be the one I had prayed for, as his qualities would line up with what God's Word teaches. First, I needed to know that this man really loved the Lord and we were on the same page. It was important that his faith had been tested and found to be true.

This friend was a very nice man who cared a lot for me, and I cared for him as well, but only as a friend, and that is where it would need to stay. My prayer for him was that his search in building a relationship with God was real; real enough for him to pursue God first and not me. I felt sure that he would be hurt, but if his wanting God in his life was real; he would seek out God on his own.

I told him that we needed to stop going out, as I thought I might be leading him on or giving him false hopes. I could not see him as anything but a friend. I tried to be gentle, comforting him by saying that our friendship had been a blessing and if that's what he needed to start going back to church and reading God's Word, then this time together had been good. I told him about Chuck Swindoll's message saying, "If God puts someone in your life, it will be someone who can walk with you and grow with you, instead of your feeling that you need to run to catch up." Then in his hurt, he said he couldn't do it without me. I told him it is a choice we all need to make on our own. It isn't a group decision. Yes, it is easier if someone you know goes to church or Bible studies with you, but I couldn't be that friend.

For that next month I tried to continue doing business with him. He had stopped going to church and the Bible study. I knew it was time to cut all ties. The seeds had been planted. I know if my focus had not been on the Lord and what He wants to do in and through my life, I could have chosen another dime, again for the wrong reason, falling back to my "savior mentality." Satan tries so hard to get us to fall in our weak areas, but this lesson had been learned as my focus was where it belonged and not on myself. Thank you, Jesus, for I would have missed the journey you had ahead for me. I would have missed this assignment of writing about the journey to give some of you reading this book the hope and encouragement that He wants to give you.

Yes, God had another plan and I could feel it. God had a special journey ahead. One that I am to share with you now; one that will give Him the honor and glory that He deserves and tells of His great love and grace for us. I just needed to trust Him, hang on and buckle up for what many times has felt like a roller coaster ride!! But, this I know, Jesus has been beside me on that ride, and as long as my focus remained on Him, I saw many victories. And when at times, I looked at the storm, or circumstances around me, (as Peter did when he stepped out of the boat to walk to Jesus,) the fears of "what if's" would come back. Then I would remember something I had read a few years back: *if you're looking at God, then He looks big enough to take care of your problems or fears, but if you look at your problems or fears, they will look bigger than God.*

3

~

Shiny Dimes

What are "shiny dimes?" *They are those in process to become one of God's best. The ones that affected me were in career choices and relationships. A "shiny dime" is not of the world, but it is shiny only as long as God is allowed to shape and polish it. It may become a dollar choice in God's time and way. It's just not there yet. A "shiny dime" may seem like a good choice, but it isn't the "best choice," not God's. He wants us to have His Best, not settle for just good or even second best, to go for His dollars.* **This is when He will receive the greater praise from our lives, and we the biggest joy.**

Chapter two ended in the winter of 1995. The manners program was going well, both in Knoxville and in some North Carolina areas. In March, I met Kristy from Charlotte who agreed to start as my class helper, observing as I taught. We would then team-teach, so I could decide if she would remain a helper or be a trained instructor I could let fly solo with some of the classes. When that time came, I knew God had answered my prayer for a special lady to help me. She was a fast learner and very good with the students.

I met Kristy through Nancy who had also taught the manners classes with my friend Kay, in Florida, as I had. Then Nancy had moved to Charlotte. I love it when we can see how God works through His people to give us answers to prayer. Kristy was young, single, full of energy, a teacher in a church school and the students loved her. We hit it off great, as we shared our love for our Lord together. Oh, how I thanked God for putting Kristy in my life, both to help me with the business and as a new and neat Christian friend. By the next set of classes, Kristy was doing the program in one store, while I was teaching at another.

In mid April between classes, I put my special Suzie in the car and drove home to Ohio for a visit. Dad's health was not doing well. He was still at home, but I felt it was important to see him and mother as often as I could. I was able to work in one more visit in August before Dad was put into the nursing home the end of September.

After my trip in April, I contacted a lady in my Bible study class at church who had expressed an interest in doing the manners classes with me in Knoxville. Liz was also a teacher who enjoyed working with students. I gave her the videos to watch and class materials to review, so we would be ready for the next set of classes the end of that month. The classes were a little smaller, but with still higher than normal numbers, good ones to train Liz. So again, God provided another good helper and instructor. She was wonderful with the students and very dependable. By mid summer, if I needed to be in another location, she would be where I needed her, doing the classes solo. We ended up being a good team, just like Kristy and me in Charlotte.

In the beginning of May, a lady in my Bible study class, started a study in her home called "Experiencing God." It was highly recommended. Mary and I made the twelve-week commitment on Tuesday nights. God used this study to speak to me, to grow my understanding of Him, and to help me hang on to Him in the times ahead when my faith was again to be stretched, almost to the limit.

The programs were now winding down before the end of the school year. My younger sister and her husband came to see one of the Knoxville graduations and spent a little time with me. It was good for some of my family to see how God was providing. They had been concerned through my marriage, the divorce, and now being on my own. Yes, they could see God's care of me. While they still didn't like seeing me alone, they were comforted.

As I had finished all the programs by mid-May and had set up the summer programs in both states, I was looking forward to visiting my friends in Texas. Craig had taken a job in a cell-group ministry type of church in Houston. (Dee and I had been friends since our time together in Bible Study Fellowship; it was Craig who gave me 1Corinthians 7:15 when I asked him where I stood Biblically, as my husband wanted a divorce.) I finally had time and was ready for some new scenery with old friends. My income had been good enough to plan the trip. Angie, a young friend who loved Suzie, was happy to watch her and my apartment.

Dee was waiting as I got off the plane in Houston. We were ready to enjoy this time together after visiting by phone and letters for over two years. I had never been to Houston and was excited to be there! At dinner that evening, I noticed an "Experiencing God" book lying on a stand and asked who was doing that study. Both Craig and Dee were. I had brought my book along. We commented on how often our lives were going through similar types of struggles or victories at the same time, and so often we would be studying or reading the same books.☺

One morning as I read my devotions, I wrote down in my journal a part that I felt God wanted me to listen to and remember. ***"When the saved soul so trusts Me and seeks no more their own way, he leaves the future to Me, its rescuer."*** The verse was Joel 2:25, which is about restoring the years the locusts have eaten. I remember thinking as I wrote it down, "But, Lord, isn't that what I am doing? Haven't I been holding loosely to any plans and letting You lead and control? Haven't I been praying through any decisions?" I asked the Lord to show me if there was any area where I still wanted my own way and to help my focus to be first and always on Him. But why the verse in Joel? Normally when I felt Jesus telling me something, what I read in His Word backed up or lined up with the thought that stood out to me. Since I didn't understand what this meant, I had tucked it away by writing it down. If the Lord were trying to tell me something, He would repeat it in another way. Then I would remember this and it would fit.

One evening as we were sitting in their family room, Dee told me about her uncle, a godly man. She got out some pictures and asked if I'd be open to meeting him. I laughed and accused her of trying to play cupid, but agreed. Her uncle Joel and I were about the same age and single. I had to admit I liked it when Dee said, "Wouldn't it be nice to be real family?" I again teased her saying "we are family." (But I knew what she meant and enjoyed the compliment.) Time passed quickly. I had enjoyed the visit. The surprise phone calls and letters from them were a real blessing, but I still prefer face to face with hugs! ☺

Mary met me at the Knoxville airport and drove me home after we stopped for dinner. She filled me in on the lesson I had missed in the "Experiencing God" study, and we shared what our Lord is showing us, how He has been with us, growing our faith. Mary has been a special friend. We have also shared about our hopes and fears and everything else that affects our lives. I have watched her faith grow so much in the time since we met, when she was just a new believer.

Less than a week after my Texas vacation, the first of the advertisements were in the Sunday papers for registration in each area. As the registrations began coming in, I became concerned as the number of students were considerably less in Knoxville and the Ashville program didn't have enough enrollment to go. Charlotte numbers were still doing well, but now I have two helper/instructors to pay, making my income less. As I looked to Jesus each day for answers, He seemed to be silent. Why? Was I missing something He was telling me? The next couple of months were tight on finances. Ruby put it best: She said it was like God had a calculator figuring out just how much I would need that month, and that is what came in, no more but no less.

June was a special month, even though the business numbers were down, and I was naturally concerned about my finances. The Bible study focused on how God speaks to us. It reminded of the ways He had spoken to me through prayer, reading His Word, His people and my circumstances. The four ways this study was teaching He does! I was seeing that as God helps us, we are to assist those behind us by helping them up the next rung of the ladder. As God tells in His Word, *"We are to comfort others behind us with the comfort that we have received from God Himself."* (2Corinthians 1:3-5) This "Experiencing God" study described it like a croquet game. First you went here, and then God took you over there. What I had missed before was how God seeing the whole picture, can see moves that we don't understand but are needed to complete His Plan. This picture made it so much clearer.

On the heels of that understanding, my counselor friend Ellen, who had invited me to stay with her when I first came back to Knoxville, and Linda who was over the women's ministry at church, asked me to take a class with them to be able to help Linda with some of the counseling needs. They knew I was busy, but each had prayed for the Lord to give them the names of the ladies whom He wanted on that list. My name was the only one that came up on both lists. Would I pray about it and let them know? Linda was overwhelmed with the number of ladies who were asking for counseling. I prayed about it and knew God was guiding me to start the class; even with all the questions I had about where He was leading me.

July came. The June programs had ended and I was now working on the fall schedule. I had one small program in July in Knoxville with a Boy Scout troop. It was a change of pace and we all had a good time. I also could do it alone, which meant I had the income now to get through to the end of August.

The National Director who had started the manners program had a yearly business meeting. So, the weekend of July 21st-23rd I flew to St. Louis. I always enjoyed going as the ladies shared what they were doing in their territories and new things that were working for them. It was also a good time to see friends in the business. Kay, my friend from Florida, would be sharing a room with her sister Kathy. Another friend of ours from Texas was sharing a room with me. The four of us stayed together during free times. My roommate Jane was at the end of a long and troubled marriage. She also loved the Lord and that was a real irritant to her husband. Oh, my, I could identify with that!

During one of the business meetings, the owner of the program said she had just gotten the Houston territory back from the previous owner and would sell it for a very low price to the regional director who would take it and run with it. Now, the room we were in was very warm, but I was sitting there with goose bumps all over me, feeling that the Lord was saying that I was to buy it, sell the ones I now owned, and move to Texas. Kathy looked down and saw the goose bumps on my arms and asked if I was all right. I said, "yes," and I would fill her in later, as she gave me a questioning look.

That evening when the four of us were together, I shared what I felt God was asking me to do: *Sell my Knoxville and North Carolina territories, and buy Houston and move there.* Why should I move to Texas? Jane got excited and said how nice it would be for both of us to be in Texas. Kay was quietly digesting it, and then said what I was thinking. "God needs to show you clearly this is what He is asking you to do." We all agreed. Later, back in our room, I told Jane about my recent trip to Houston and about Dee wanting me to meet her uncle. Of course, as we gals do, we spoke about some "what if's," and why had the business slowed down in Knoxville? When we place our lives in our Lord's Hands, we need to have our seat belts on and hang on, as we don't know which direction He will take us next.☺

On the flight home, my mind was drifting across all that was happening. I thought about the lessons that I knew God had been showing me in the "Experiencing God" Bible study that I had just finished. *"Watch to see where God is working and join Him. Listen for His Voice and be willing to go where He asks you to go."* My focus needs to be on God, not my life. Be moldable and remain at God's disposal to be used as He chooses.

Ruby was waiting at the airport. I told her how I felt upon hearing the Houston territory was for sale. She smiled and said, "I knew God was going to move you to Texas." Then I

remembered a little over a year ago as I was struggling with wanting to move back to Orlando, I had shown Ruby a video of a church service there. I told her how I was hoping I could move back. Out of the blue she had said, "No, I think you are to come back to Tennessee for a while, but then, I think God is going to take you to Texas." By this time, I'm in tears saying, "Why would I want to move to Texas?" Ruby said, "I don't know. That's what I felt God was leading me to say and I just spit it out." As I told Ruby I was remembering that, she laughed while saying, "Oh yes, she remembered it, too." We spent some time discussing that possibility. Then I said, "But why would I feel so strongly that He wanted me to do the classes with Ellen and Linda for the training I need to help Linda with counseling the ladies at the church?" Ruby said, "I feel you are to do the classes also, but God will use your training wherever He has you living when He is ready."

The advertisements would be starting for the fall programs the third week in August. As soon as I had all the paperwork in place, I decided to make another trip home, as Dad was not doing well. I knew once the fall programs began, there would be no time to get away. I was feeling concerned about the slow down in the numbers for the program, but as I read God's Word each morning, my devotions and Scripture reading kept encouraging me. One day a word of encouragement came from my devotional by saying ***"God never leads me where His Grace will not keep me."*** Another day as I read Acts 10:16-25, I knew the Lord was telling me *"God chooses what we go through, but I must choose how I will go through it."*

I did not want my family to know about my concern over

the lower enrollment numbers, which had lowered my income, nor was I ready to share the possibility of the Lord leading me to move to Texas. They also didn't need to hear how lonely I had begun to feel, wanting that special one to share life with instead of the business being my life. All were concerned about Dad right now and didn't need to worry about me. I was just in one of those "uncomfortable times" of not knowing what was ahead or what I was to do. Besides, I knew the Lord was going to take care of me. One of the hard lessons He had needed to teach me is I do not need to know what is ahead. My job is to keep my focus on Him and trust Him. **Only God knows what lies ahead. I am to trust, knowing I am safe in His Hand.** But that's a hard one! And, if I were to make a guess, I would say that is probably a lesson that most of you have a hard time with also. It's so natural to want to see what is ahead and to feel you're in control of what is to happen.

I had just gotten home from my visit with Mom and Dad, and taken Suzie for a nice long walk. My mind was on how much Dad's health had slipped in the short time since mid April. As I reached my apartment, I took a deep breath and said out loud, **"Oh Lord, what does lie ahead for me?"** I gave Suzie a treat as we sat down to watch the news before bedtime. The phone rang. It was too late for business calls and my friends usually didn't call after 10:00pm. There was a man's voice that I didn't know, explaining he was sorry to be calling so late. He had written a letter to me, then felt God said, "No, pick up the phone and introduce yourself to her instead." He was Dee's Uncle Joel. We had a good time visiting, and some laughs at how Dee wanted us to meet. To be honest, I didn't think he would ever call, as it was three months since Dee started working on this. Long distance makes it hard to keep a relationship going, but never having met, we were at square one. So we agreed to take turns calling and writing and see what happens.

It was now the third week in August and the registration for my fall classes were just beginning. Along with the regular classes of the two in Knoxville, three in Charlotte, and one in Ashville, I was adding a new program in Winston-Salem, North Carolina. I would be adding one in Greensboro also, but not until early spring. I was to meet with a young lady who lived in the Winston-Salem area. She was also a teacher and had expressed an interest in helping me in that area, plus Ashville and Greensboro.

Building the Business

Most people think working a manners business is easy. What they don't realize is that I had sixteen-hour days, endless hours making and returning phone calls and unending paperwork. From the beginnings of setting up a program to following it all the way through until that set was complete. Now keep in mind; I didn't do just one set, then wait on the next. This was my income. To live on it, I needed to overlap programs, which made it "real interesting." I could be getting supplies for the second class at one location, buying roses for the graduation for a different class, and doing the registration to begin another program somewhere else, all at the same time!!

Can you picture this yet? When I added my assistants to the mix, there were even more programs to schedule with all the work for each PLUS I now had payroll to do. I was so tired at the end of each day I just fell into bed, exhausted. The best picture I can give you of my life through these years is; **I was like the juggler in the circus who starts by spinning a couple of plates on some pegs, then keeps adding more plates while needing to keep all of them spinning and not daring to let one fall!!** That is why at holiday times, I needed down time to see family or friends and <u>recuperate</u>!

My plate was FULL! Not only were the fall registrations going on, but I was also taking classes with Ellen and Linda. There was homework that needed to be done. Then Linda asked me to do a special program in September for the women. It was a "reaching out" ministry where women in the church would invite friends and neighbors who didn't go to church. There was a dinner along with a choice of classes. My talk on table manners and dinner table settings was one of the sideshows (as I dubbed them.) ☺ Little did I know what God was going to do through this for me!

How I cherished "time outs" with my friends. One day I asked Ruby, "Do you think I will ever have a 'regular' home life? One with a good husband, who loves the Lord, loves me and wants to take care of me? Don't get me wrong, for I am very thankful for how my Heavenly Father is taking care of me. I just get so tired sometimes at the pace I'm going and wonder how long I can keep it up: The not-knowing-what's-ahead-feeling as if I'm on a roller coaster. Sometimes I see God's Hand so clearly as He opens the way miraculously. The business has me running at times to keep up; other times, I don't see any clear direction and barely make enough to get by as money gets tight."

I learned how to make four meals from a can of tuna, or several meals from a small pot roast or pot of chili. Sometimes when I was so busy, I baked a sweet potato in the microwave and took bites between phone calls or ran around my apartment doing paperwork with it on a napkin in my hand. Ruby called a few times in the afternoons to see how I was doing. After hearing for the second or third time that I was carrying my baked sweet potato lunch around, she would laugh just picturing me.☺ That's how I have eaten many meals and survived many a day since doing this business. Oh, my students should have seen me: Miss Manners as I was called on one of the local radio stations by a host who had me on his show a couple of times. But then, my approach to the students was that they didn't always need to act like a lady, but that it is important for them to know how to act when the time is appropriate.

The fall classes began. The numbers were above average with forty to fifty in the Knoxville area, and about the same in the North Carolina programs. The new program in Winston-Salem went well, and I hired the young lady I had talked with from that area. She was also to help with the Ashville program in October. During this time, I received a call from one of the ladies who worked with the "Lady Vols" at the University of Tennessee. She had read in the church bulletin about the program I was to teach at the ladies ministry on "table manners." Remember my statement "little did I know what God was going to do through this for me?" After two meetings, I was hired to work with all of the women's sports teams. What a financial blessing and it came just before the holidays, a normally slow time in the business!

The third week of October, I drove home for Dad's funeral. Liz was teaching a class that Saturday in Knoxville, Kristy was teaching in Charlotte, while I had a class in Ashville. Angie came to stay with Suzie. Dad's funeral was on Sunday. As much as I hated to leave Mother so soon, I needed to drive back on Monday, as that was the evening I was to start the program for the Lady Vols. I got home with just enough time to change into a nice suit and arrive on time. That first meeting was an over-view of the program with all one hundred and fifty students and it went well, as did all of the following classes with the different teams. How I thanked my Lord for this blessing as I had really enjoyed the change AND it had brought my income back up to normal.

The holidays were quickly approaching and all of the fall programs had gone well. The air was getting crisp for Suzie's morning walks, but we both appreciated the slow-down in my schedule. I had been enjoying cards, flowers and calls from Dee's uncle Joel over the past couple of months. Also, I did have a couple of blind dates that a friend set up for me. Though he was nice, we didn't click with things in common. Another man from church had shown interest as we shared some time over coffee and walks. I could easily have fallen for him and knew the feelings were mutual. But, even though we enjoyed our few times together and had been through a lot of the same things, which made a bond of understanding, I felt God softly saying, "No." In one of our talks, I told him about the possibility of God moving me to Texas and also about my friend's uncle who had been calling. He knew about the classes I had been taking to be able to help Linda, the ladies' pastor. He also was aware of my growing territories in the business. However, I told him I knew God was telling me to hold everything with an open hand as I watched for His leading. He understood that I had loved his heart for the Lord's work and had even asked, "Why not Lord? This could be good!" *But God gave me silence.* Sometimes God will answer that "why" question, but most of the time, we get silence. He had said no, now I was to trust knowing He knew what was best. My heart still ached as this man began to date another lady.

One morning my Scripture reading was Psalm 84. **Growing strong in God's presence is often preceded by a journey through barren places in our lives.** I knew God had me on a journey, a journey that was to stretch and grow my faith along with honoring Him. Maybe my journey still had some more bends in the road ahead and more hills to climb. I needed to continue placing my life in His hand each day.

Thanksgiving was a little over two weeks away. Mother was not ready to have a big dinner this soon after Dad's passing away. I had been invited to visit the Lanes in Texas. Mom said that was fine. She knew I needed a break after the busy fall schedule. I made the arrangements with the Lanes and got a ticket for a good price. Dee told me her uncle Joel was going to try to be there also. Within a couple of days, he phoned himself to say he would be able to make it.

I could hardly believe it: another visit to Houston in just over six months. Dee was excited that her uncle and I would finally meet. He arrived later that evening with a couple of his daughters. After communicating long distance for three months, we felt like good friends. The next day, I could see why he had enjoyed being a youth pastor as we spent time playing on the trampoline with some of the kids. A couple of days later, he asked me to go with him to a college in Houston that he had been talking with about a job. That would move him to Houston. He also plays tennis, which was a plus, and yes, he really does love the Lord, the main plus. We all had a good time and there was never a dull moment! The days flew! It was soon time to fly back home.

During the next three weeks I worked at lining up the programs to begin toward the end of January. In fact, I had all of the programs set in both states until the end of May. I had promised my son that I would be able to visit during the Christmas holidays. When I told my long-distance friend, Joel, I would be going to Orlando for Christmas, he worked it out to be there for three days, as he had a college friend that he could stay with.

Christmas time was a good break and the last before Easter. My son was working on Christmas day, so I went with my friend Joel to his sister's to meet more of his family. The next day we visited with his college friend and family. We had enjoyed our time together, but my friend needed to go back home to Texas. The week before, the college in Houston offered him a job beginning in late January. It was clear God was working out his move. Now I was watching to see what He had ahead for me. I stayed in Orlando through New Year's Day, giving me more time for my son and other friends. On the flight home, my mind was spinning with questions of how would God show me His direction. Ruby met me at the airport. We spent some time over a late lunch, as she wanted to know how things had gone. It felt good to be home. Suzie was really glad to see me as I promised her we would have more time together now. ☺

It was the first week of January in 1996. My friend Joel and I had resumed the phone calling. He would soon ask me to marry him. I agreed "IF" the Lord moved both of us to Houston and continued to show us that He was leading us to get married. Our Lord now had Joel's job worked out. I contacted the lady who owned the manners' program to see if anyone had bought the Houston territory yet. She still had it and was excited that I was thinking about it. I would keep in touch and let her know if I was interested. I would need to sell the territories in Tennessee and North Carolina first. I was depending on God to either provide buyers quickly and easily so I would know if this was in His Plan for me, or to close the doors. I wanted to be where He wanted me, but was getting nervous about the possibility of His asking me to start over in Texas. I learned that the department store I was doing the manners classes with in Tennessee and North Carolina, which had been so receptive to the program and me, had not been to the previous Houston territory director. **I needed to KNOW it was God's leading before I made the move.**

That next week, the snow started. My first winter in the Knoxville area was the worst in over 100 years. This winter would beat that one!☹ (Remember, I'm the one who loved Florida because I hate winter.) While I was snowed in the next four days, and thankful I had just stocked up on groceries, I called to visit with Liz. She was home from school due to the snow days, so I filled her in about the possibility of my moving to Texas. When I asked if she would be interested in buying and running the Knoxville territory, she was excited, but also needed time to think about it. I told her I would not be selling it until after this next set, and only if at that time I had a buyer for at least one of my North Carolina territories. That would be the only way I would know God was in the move. When I had asked Kristy if she was interested in the Charlotte territory, she quickly said, "No." Then I would offer it to Nancy. Kristy stated if Nancy bought it, she would continue to work for her, so I made the call to Nancy. She was excited about it and would discuss it with her husband.

January and February were long weeks of being hammered with snow and cold weather. By the first week in February, the program numbers were good in Knoxville, Charlotte, and the new territory in Greensboro. However, the first classes in two stores needed to be rescheduled due to snow, which meant doubling up on the next classes to end the programs on time. I was feeling extremely stressed. Then Joel called. Since his job had started in Houston, he was living with the Lanes. We weren't into our conversation but a couple of minutes when Joel said he felt I was dragging my feet on moving to Houston, and we had our first argument. I told him I wasn't going to just "walk away" from this business the Lord had given me unless I knew it was in His plan. If I were to move to Houston, then I was sure God would bring buyers for my territories. But Joel felt God was going to move me to Houston, as he had him, for us to be together. Even though our relationship had been going well, I wasn't that sure, and was waiting for God's leading and timing, not wanting to take any detours on the way.

By mid February, Nancy and her husband had decided not to buy the Charlotte territory. I prayed, "OK Lord, are you closing the door? Does this mean I am to stay here and not move to Houston?" I had just finished the classes with Ellen and Linda and would be able to help with the counseling ministry if I stayed. When I looked at what a job it would be to move and start over, I felt relieved. Then I wondered, but why did I feel so strongly I was to buy the Houston territory and move? The phone rang and it was Kristy, my instructor in Charlotte. She was so excited. Her dad was going to loan her the money to buy that territory. She now felt God had put it in her heart to buy it. By that weekend, I had driven to Charlotte to meet with Kristy and her dad; the paperwork was completed. Liz had decided to buy the Knoxville area. She would take the program over after the March set was completed. My paperwork had arrived to buy the Houston territory a couple of weeks earlier, for if and when I was ready for it. I felt like I had gotten caught up in a "whirlwind." I knew now that God was sending me to Texas! Joel was so happy as we both watched how quickly our Lord was clearing the path ahead and was moving me to Houston, too. So, at his prompting, we set a wedding date. My family and friends were having mixed feelings as they were excited with me but worried for me as well.

March was a month of "letting go." That first Saturday was my last class and graduation in Greensboro. I had advertised to sell that territory, which included the Winston-Salem area, but nothing so far. The young lady who had started as a helper was now engaged and not interested in owning the business. At the end of the graduation, I asked the audience if anyone was interested or knew of someone who may be to see me as soon as the stage was cleared. Four ladies stopped by. One lady picked up a business flier and said she may call. Her daughter had been in the program and loved it. Liz would be taking over any new programs in Knoxville that I had scheduled and the same with Kristy for Charlotte. I had two more programs set up for me to do: one in Ashville and the last one back in Winston-Salem after Easter break and ending May 1st. Again, Joel was not happy about this, as he thought I should be moving sooner.

Then I received a call from Dee in Houston. She had been gathering information on apartments as I would fly there during Easter to begin looking for a place to call home. She could find no apartments that would allow a big dog like Suzie. Joel had found the same answer. As I prayed about this, I felt God was saying, *"It's time to let go of Suzie."* "But, Lord, she has been my buddy for over six and a half years, and you gave her to me! How can I leave her? How can I find a home for her? She's middle-aged and beginning to have arthritis in her hips. Lord, this is the hardest thing You have ever asked me to do!" My heart was breaking as I pled with the Lord to help me find a place in Texas that would let me keep her. Yet somehow I knew God would work it out in a special way if I was to give up Suzie.

I asked my Bible study class to please pray with me that

74

God would provide the perfect home for Suzie, where they would love her unconditionally, but would still give me visiting privileges. I wanted Suzie to remember me but be content to stay with her new owners. That would be a tall order and it needed to be answered within a week or two.

Well, I want you to know, God had a home all ready for her, and she was in it five days later. My Bible study group still marvels at how quickly and completely God answered that prayer. I stayed away for three weeks, giving Suzie time to bond with her new parents. When I went back to see her, she was all excited to see me. I took her for a walk and talked with her like we did before. When it came time to go, I loved on her and told her to be a good girl for me, while she gave me another kiss. Then she went over and stood with her new mom while giving that pretty swish with her fluffy tail, like she knew this was where she belonged and was telling me it was OK. I sobbed all the way home, but knew she was going to be just fine. God had worked out a miracle for both of us. Her new daddy is well known in the Knoxville area. Today, he won't let them put his picture in the paper unless Suzie is in the picture with him.☺ They even had my dog sitter Angie sit for them on several occasions. Isn't God good! Even Ruby was blown away with that answer! She has taken me to visit Suzie on several of my visits back to that area and has said, "God took Suzie to doggy heaven early. They treat her even better than you did!" And, after that, any time I would get concerned about how my life was going, Ruby would always say, ***"If God took care of Suzie like He has, He is going to take care of you."*** ☺

The next week I drove up to spend some time with my

mother. We had a good visit as it snowed us in the last two days. We popped corn and played some of Mom's favorite games. I knew at this point God was taking me to Houston, which would mean longer times between visits. I would not be able to hop in the car in the morning and be there later that afternoon. I thanked God for this special time my mother and I had together. I even slept with her a couple of those nights as we talked and laughed until one of us fell asleep. Sweet memories. ☺

When I got back to my apartment, I had a message from the lady who had picked up a flyer in Greensboro. She had talked with her husband about buying the territory. They were interested and ready to talk. We set up a time to meet. They had prayed about it and felt God was leading her to do this program. Another of God's people! I told her about Kristy in Charlotte and said I knew they would be able to help each other, as their territories were next to one another. I knew they would hit it off well. Wow! In less than a month, God had sold three of my territories, and found a great home for Suzie.

The beginning of the next week, I flew to Houston. There was a "Family Life" marriage conference that next weekend, and Joel wanted us to go as an engaged couple. I agreed as it looked like God was leading us to be together. This conference was a good test. The main goal of my first three days was to find an apartment. I went out with Dee and was feeling pretty discouraged as nothing in my price range even came close to my apartment in Knoxville. The areas didn't look good or the apartments were small. I needed a two bedroom with a den for an office. Joel went out with me the second evening, but most of their offices were closed. He gave me a list that an apartment finder had given him. The last afternoon we had to look, Dee and I went out together. She pointed to one on the list, but I said, "Let's check this one out first." It was a mess. We were discouraged. We stopped and prayed. We had only enough time to check the one we had passed up. When we went into the office, knowing their prices were higher, I just asked if they had any two-bedroom apartments and what was the price. The price was at the top of my range. As the lady was taking me to see the floor plan, I said that I really needed an extra room for an office, but couldn't afford more. She said, "Oh, they just put the two-bedroom with a den on special twenty minutes ago." It was one dollar "under" my top dollar! When we stepped in to see the floor plan, I said, "This is it!" It was 1400 sq.ft. The den for my office was behind the living room, with a nice big window. If we had looked at it any sooner, the office girl would not even have known about the special. Thank you, Lord! I later realized how central the Lord had placed me for the business. I had easy access to all the main roads within minutes.

The weekend came quickly and with it the marriage conference. We were in with the married couples for all parts except one for engaged couples only. Toward the end, they asked us to look at each other and tell him or her you are ready for a life commitment; then switch. Well, he went first and talked and talked. I was getting more and more nervous as I knew I could not say that. **Something was wrong, but I didn't know what.** Finally, they said, "Time's up." I gave a sigh of relief as he was apologizing for talking too much. I said,

"That's OK." I couldn't even share this with Dee. She was so excited that I was moving close to them again and was to marry her uncle.

That Sunday I flew home. Tuesday, I wrote in my journal, "Though I know God sold the territories, gave Suzie a good home, and now has given me the perfect apartment in Houston, something is wrong." **I had lost my joy and that scared me.** I prayed for the Lord to show me what was wrong. The next day my Scripture reading was James 5:13-18. The thought for the day was *"make it a point to pinpoint your prayers, focus on specific requests."* Then my devotional reading went on to say, *"I am here, your waiting Lord, bring Me into everything."*

I spent as much time with my Knoxville friends as I could, as my moving date was May 2nd. I knew God was moving me to Houston so why would I hang on to Knoxville? My territories were gone, so I had no job here, and my precious dog was placed in another home. **Yet, why could I almost smell the rubber burning on the heels of my shoes from putting the brakes on?** I knew I was not looking forward to the many long hours of setting up the business and finding new ways to market the program since the department store company I had been dealing with had not been receptive to hosting the program in Houston. In fact, I was quite nervous about how long it could take for income to live on. The revenue from the Ashville and Winston-Salem programs was the cushion to pay for the move and the first two month's rent; then I needed to be earning some income. I had paid off my car, making me debt free, with the sale of the Knoxville territory. This was a very hard time for me, who until a couple of years ago always had a job with enough income, and regular income, that I could count on and not worry. These past few years, I knew in my heart God had been stretching my faith, but there were times when in my mind, I was screaming as the date for bills to be paid was close as was my checking account. It was a fearful time for this lady. *The Lord was so patient as He pointed out in His Word that I wasn't to be fearful. He said, stop looking at all of the "what if's" and look back in your journey at how I have been with you, taking care of you!*

We were now in the middle of April and the cold winter with snow was still hanging on. I really missed Suzie, my buddy. My apartment was lonely without her and my walks were never the same. That Friday was a cold, blustery day. I lingered over God's Word longer that morning and spent more time in prayer as I was in a low mode. I began listening to a new tape Ruby had given me. A pastor was teaching on Is. 43:18-19. ***"Forget the former things; do not dwell on the things of the past. See, I am doing a new thing! Now it springs up, do you not see it? I am making a way in the desert and streams in the wasteland."*** Those words stuck with me for days! I was reminded of the dream that Ruby had a short time ago. We were on a trip together, and when we reached a certain place in Texas, I knew this was where I was to get out. All around me, it was green, like an oasis. Around that, it was brown. Was this the new place God had for me? Was the Lord going to make a place in this desert for me?

The next day I visited with Ellen, my counselor friend in Knoxville. I told her about how God was clearing the path ahead for my move to Houston. Then, I told her I felt my joy was gone. Was it due to fear of "what if's?" The Lord had opened the doors! She asked me about this man I had agreed to marry. He sounded like a good person. Then she said, ***"WAIT until all lights are green with no caution or red lights before getting married."*** I agreed to do that. I had already moved the wedding date out later than Joel had wanted.

Both Ruby and Mary had come over to help me pack. My apartment was not looking very homey, so I was glad I was driving to Orlando for a few days to see my son and friends there, as I didn't know when I would make it back after moving to Houston. My friends in Orlando are so special. They have prayed me through the dying marriage and on to the time of being on my own, starting and growing a business, and now this. I have fewer friends in Knoxville, but each one, God placed in my life at just the right time, being just as special. I wondered what friends God would give me in Houston? The Ashville program was completed now. I would need to be back in Knoxville to start the last class in Winston-Salem, and then the move.

My Bible study class came over to say goodbye and I was on my way. The past couple of days had been filled with tearful goodbyes, and, of course, another visit with Suzie. With Knoxville behind me and Houston in front of me, all I could say over and over as the rented truck wheels rolled me down the road was "my life is in Your Hand, Lord."

Houston Bound

I arrived in Houston on Saturday, May 4th. With the help of Craig and Dee, their three children, plus, of course, my fiancé Joel, and a couple from the church, the apartment was beginning to look somewhat livable by bedtime. The next morning was church and a good day to be thankful for the safe trip and what He had ahead for me here.

The next week I called the department store company I had been dealing with before. They had moved their headquarters and some of the staff recently, so they wanted to hear about the program I was teaching. They asked me to fax all the information to them. I asked the apartment office if I could receive a fax there. The lady in charge agreed. Then she asked about my business. After I explained it to her, she said she was impressed. Then added, "If you need to run copies, send or receive a fax, as long as we aren't using the machines, you are welcome to use them." (They had allowed me to do that at my apartment in Knoxville, but at a charge.) The whole time that I lived at the apartment in Houston, I knew God had shown me favor, as they let me use the office freely at no charge.

I didn't let any grass grow under my feet on the business. The business needed to produce an income for rent and food quickly! While I waited on an answer from the department store chain I had dealt with in Knoxville and North Carolina, I was checking out other possibilities. I did get a class set up for the beginning of summer in a career center, just a one day over-view type of program, but I was thankful for it. Then the refund check from my apartment in Knoxville came earlier than expected. Next I got a call from the district office of the department store that I had faxed information to. To my surprise, they were interested! They were going to email all of the managers in their stores to let them know I would be contacting them. Talk about a stamp of approval! When the headquarters of a company does that, it's like they just rolled out the red carpet for you. Then I asked, "Who do I work the scheduling through?" I knew that had previously been a problem in Houston. Surprisingly, the lady on the phone said there had been a woman in charge of their 'special events,' but she has been let go. You will be setting up the schedules directly with the managers. Then I asked, "Can you tell me when this change was made?" She gave me the date. It was on Saturday, May 4th, the same day I drove into town. Is that not God? How much clearer could He have made it; He was clearing the way for me again. I was off and running with more stores to host my program than I had in both Knoxville and North Carolina territories put together.

Now to catch you up on what was happening in my personal life during this same two weeks. In my time with the Lord over and over again, He was telling me, ***"Stand firm, stand still, do not be afraid, you will see the deliverance I will bring you."*** When Joel and others confronted me about why I wasn't working on plans for the wedding, I said I had been too busy getting the business started. But, I knew if a bride-to-be was excited and ready for her marriage that would be her first priority. Did I have "cold feet" or was God telling me something?

Then Dee called and asked me to pray about something.

The Christian magazine she worked for had just hired a young lady to be assistant editor. She was to fly in the end of the month. They could not find a place for her to rent as she didn't want more than a three-month lease and could not afford to pay a lot. Would I be willing to rent out my second bedroom? As I prayed, I knew God was saying she was to be my roommate. When I shared this with Joel, he was upset. He didn't want a renter with us after we were married. Again I took this to the Lord in prayer. Then when I opened my Bible praying for direction, God showed me a certain verse. It was NOT in His plan for me to get married at this time. He had brought me to Houston for another purpose. All of the hesitation I had felt in my heart, all of the concerns that I had been seeing, and the feeling I'd had at the marriage conference, all made sense now as God showed me in His Word this special verse. I knew that evening when Joel came over I needed to share with him what I knew God had told me: We needed to cancel the wedding. My journey with my Lord was not over, and my fiancé had a journey of his own to take care of. He was a good man, a godly man, but he had some issues to work on before he was ready for marriage.

A year ago when Dee thought her uncle and I might be good together, I made an entry in my journal. It was *"when the saved soul so trusts Me and seeks no more their own way, he leaves the future to Me, its rescuer."* In the two weeks prior to canceling the wedding, while spending more time in God's Word, my Lord was telling me to stand still, don't be afraid, you will see the deliverance the Lord will bring you. I understood it now; and **He had delivered me with His Word. I may have**

missed it, if I had not been in His Word and listening for His voice to lead me. Yes, God was preparing me for a move to Houston, but not a marriage. It was time to move on, looking forward to what God was doing now in this journey. So I picked up the phone and called the young lady who was also praying about whether she was to be my roommate. She felt very sure this was God's answer for her. We hit it off great and the three months turned into a year.☺

My family was to fly in that next week. They had known for a couple of weeks I wasn't sure about getting married at this time, but they still planned on flying down. In fact, they said not to get married unless I was sure. They all got to meet Joel, now friend, and they liked him, but they felt the same sense of relief I did about our not getting married, as God had shown me that was not in His plan. The time came for my older sister, her husband and our mother to fly home. They left in the morning and my new roommate flew in that afternoon, so my younger sister and husband would meet her and spend a couple of days with both of us before they returned home. I felt like I had been running a bed and breakfast!☺ But, I was glad for the time with my family. And, **my joy was back, as I knew I had kept my focus on the Lord.** It would have been so easy to take this detour. It looked like God was putting us together, but in my spirit, I lost my joy; His signal to me that it wasn't what He had for me.

One of the head pastors at Craig's church said it best. "God used me to help my friend see he had some work that God wanted him to do, and God used him to make the move to Houston easier for me." We were thinking, too soon, that God might be putting us together for marriage.

In this chapter, I have shown you several "shiny dimes" that I could easily have chosen if I had not been following close enough to the Lord to see the detours, or to hear Him saying, "No, not yet, it's time to move on with Me." Yes, my friend was a shiny dime in process, but so was the business that God had given me the past two years. If I had stayed in Knoxville, even though God had blessed me there, I would have been settling for less than His Best. And even with my special Suzie. What if I would have refused to give her up? God had given her to me for that 6 1/2-year season, but He now had a better plan even for her, far better than I could ever have dreamed possible. If I had stayed, I would have settled for a journey short of where God wanted me to be. Would He have taken care of me there? Would He have used me there? I think so, but for Him to get all the praise from my journey that He wanted, and for me to get all the joy He wanted to give to me, I must trudge on.

As we end this part of my journey, I feel lead to give you some words from Isaiah 41. The Lord tells us; *"Do not fear, for I am with you; do not be dismayed, for I am your God. I will strengthen you and help you. I will uphold you with my righteous right hand...For I am the Lord your God, who takes hold of your right hand and says to you, do not fear; I will help you...But you will rejoice in the Lord and glory in the Holy One of Israel."* Then He says things He will do and adds, *"So that people may see and know, may consider and understand, that the hand of the Lord has done this."* On this last line, I feel sure He means that with our lives as well.

As we allow Him to crush us, refine us as silver, and reshape us, the world will see His Handiwork in us and know that He is God. There can be nothing greater to come from our lives, than for others to be drawn to Him, our Lord and Savior, because of what they see of Him in us.

4

Tarnished Dimes

Tarnished dimes are those who were once shiny dimes, but now are tarnished by having stepped back into the world's mindset. We already said "just dimes" represent people or things of the world, and "shiny dimes" are those who are walking with the Lord, but are still in process, so not quite where God wants them to be. On my journey, I also found those who at one time had started to walk with the Lord, but now are not. These dimes have usually acquired enough head knowledge about spiritual things to be dangerous to others and themselves. They compartmentalize their lives, only giving God the parts they choose. For example, they can go to church, looking and sounding good, but the draw of the world is stronger than wanting to be in God's Will. How do they, or any of

us get there? By making wrong choices. At first,
probably just small compromises, choosing the world's
way knowing God is not pleased. To put it simply, it's
choosing what the flesh wants over what God wants.

It is time to begin walking through the next part of my journey.
It takes place during my first year living in Houston. It was a
time of seeing God's hand blessing my business even more than
He had in Tennessee. **It was also a time of loneliness, and
despair as I was disheartened with what I found in the
dating world. Tarnished dimes were not the exception, but
the rule.**

It is now the end of May in 1996. I was flying out that
afternoon to go to the annual business meeting, just hours after
my sis and her hubby left for home. My new roommate would
have the apartment to herself until I returned Sunday afternoon.
I was envious, as I needed some rest.☺ I again shared a room
with Jane and had a great reunion. Kristy came from Charlotte
with her husband and we had some time together. She was
surprised about the cancelled wedding, but also saw God's
protection over me. We praised God as I told her how He was
clearing the path in my business. Jane was trying to sell her
territory to start the Austin territory. That would put us only a
couple of hours apart!

June was a month of God showing me His care. The first
week I met with four of the store managers and scheduled two
summer programs and a couple for September. As the business
was looking good here, I couldn't help but remember the dream
my encourager friend Ruby had related to me. It felt like I had

stepped out into a green, fertile oasis! During June I did the overview of my program with the Career Center, earning my first income in Houston and was paid rent by my roommate. The month was flying. Dee and I shared over lunches as we had in Orlando. My roommate Tina was getting settled in both at home and work. We were enjoying our time together, praising God for all of His answers to our prayers and His care. Our kitchen seemed to be our praise room, either because it was bright and cheery or because she loved the flavored coffee I made.☺ We had a good time getting to know each other through heart to heart talks, going to the movies and, of course, the things we women do best, eating and shopping together.

One day after Tina and I prayed, I told her about my heart's desire for a godly man to one day share my life. She gave me Hebrews 10:32-36. In my application Bible, I found verses 35-38 interesting. ***"Endurance shows faith. Rest in what God has done and trust Him now and in the future. Our endurance shows our faith is real."*** I could see that God had blessed me with another encourager friend. He even put her right into my apartment. For Tina, I was the mother figure (plus friend) relationship she was missing at this time. Isn't God good!

By the third week in June, my fall schedule was totally filled, and I was now booking programs for after the first of the year. I needed a printer to work with me on the store flyers, signs and confirmation letters. Both Dee and Tina pointed me to just the right couple. They were a sweet, sweet couple and their faces shone with their love for our Lord. They took me under their wings, doing all they could for me, even cheering me on in the business. I know they prayed for me many times, mostly when I was dealing with a lonely heart.

By the end of June, Tina had gotten a little red car she named "Happy." She convinced me to name my car, so I called her "Angel," saying she's white and she flies.☺ That white Honda Accord with blue interior and blue pin stripes had been an answer to prayer. The best part of the blessing was not the car, but the Lord showing how much He wanted to be part of every area in my life.

Both Tina and I knew that we needed to get plugged into a church. We had been visiting two different churches together; she ended up choosing one church, while I chose the other. The one I chose was more like mine in Orlando that I loved. With this church, I could choose one of several classes and even different times, which fit my work schedule better. They also had a fitness center, so I joined the aerobic classes going three or four mornings a week.

Tina's life was getting busier also, as she was making friends at work and church. But we still had time to share and an occasional outing. Dee told me that Tina would wait for when I left the apartment to get her ice cream out to eat it out of the carton. Since I taught table manners, she thought I wouldn't approve, I guess. We laughed as I said, "I'll take care of that." That evening, while Tina and I were talking, I walked to the refrigerator, got out my ice cream and a spoon and started to eat from the container as I continued to talk. Tina got a funny look on her face; and then she started to laugh. Then I laughed as I confessed why I did it, and that I wanted her to feel comfortable.

July was busy with the two sets of over-flowing classes. I quickly started to look for a helper or two. I tried a couple, but working evenings and Saturdays seemed to be a hardship for them. Even though I was occupied, I felt very alone. I hadn't made any friends at church yet. Everyone seemed to be busy when I had time during the day, and they already had their friends. I had been here before, but God had always brought the right friends at just the right times. But now, I was feeling the pain of loneliness. Tina was working long days. Dee's life was busy being a pastor's wife, rearing three children and her job. We managed to have lunch one day a week, and we enjoyed that, but it was only one hour. I began spending more time with God and in His Word again, trying to see what direction I was to go and to hear His Voice. One week the thought in my journal was *"because I am Yours, I am never alone."* I know Lord; it's just that lonely place in my heart that's giving me a hard time again.

I began to attend functions with the singles at church, but found it was not easy to get connected. Remember, up until a couple of years ago, I had been married for quite a few years. Dating had changed a lot since I was there before. The men who talked with me and wanted to go out for lunch or dinner were not great in number. However, I began a new rule: to meet the first time at a restaurant and go Dutch. That way, there was no pressure on either of us as we "checked each other out." My car was there for a quick get-away.☺ It was during this time I saw mostly tarnished dimes, guys who walked with the world six days of the week, while giving God only Sunday (at best,) and even that was part of their social life.

One day, during my time with the Lord, I read from <u>My</u> <u>Utmost for His Highest</u>: *"God gives us a vision. Then takes us down to the valley to batter us into the shape of that vision."* **It's in the valleys many give up...Every God-given vision will become real if we will only have patience.** "Yes, Lord," I said, as I felt I had been given two visions. One was to minister to hurting women. The other was to be married to a man who loves the Lord and me and to have a godly marriage. But if either was in God's plan for me, I wanted it to be by His leading.

That same week, as I read God's Word, I came upon a favorite verse, Jeremiah 29:11: *"For I know the plans I have for you, declares the Lord, not to harm you, but to give you hope and a future."* God had given me that one to hang on to several times during my journey years. Then I read in Jeremiah 18:1-6, where the pot He was shaping was marred in His Hands. So the potter shaped it into another pot, shaping it as seemed best to Him. Too often we want to take back the control of our life, which is like telling our Heavenly Father how we want our pot to be shaped (or our life to go.) We certainly will not resemble one of God's children unless we allow Him to shape us. **It is only as we yield to Him, He begins reshaping us into valuable vessels.**

My encourager friend Ruby sent a poem God had given her. Since she was driving at the time, she needed to pull off the road to write it down. God had said it was for me.

Oh, my precious "little one"
Down hard roads you have come.
On your seas have been many storms,
And Satan meant it all for harm.

But in God's hand, you did rest
Through every trial and every test
Did you know this is the way
God makes beauty from the clay?

Round and round on His wheel you went
Looking back—it was time well spent.
When in the oven of adversity you baked,
God would whisper, "I won't forsake."

Through the years God made the clay
Into a golden vase—where grace will stay
In this vase—His Word and faith towers
Just like fresh, fragrant flowers.

Oh "little one" now always stand tall
As you share your story with all
And say to those who God still shapes,
"Wait on Him child—just wait."

Speak to those weary on your way
Tell them, "God is still molding their clay"
Encourage, "That they too shall be"
"A golden vase—someday—like me!"

Even though I know God has been molding me, I still feel pretty "cracked" most of the time. My prayer is that God will use this vessel by shining His Light through those cracks, drawing others to Himself. I thanked God for giving me these encouraging words through my friend.

My summer programs were completed by the middle of August, and I had the fall programs and their advertisements all ready to go. This was a good time to fly to Orlando and spend time with my son and some friends. When I was in Houston and not running with the business, I had too much time to think about where my life was going, or maybe not going? I was still reeling with the disappointment that the relationship I had thought might be here for me was not to be. Sometimes, alone in my apartment, I would cry out to the Lord saying, **"There has got to be more to life than just the job.** Why am I here? Of all the places I've ever lived, I am the least connected to the church here than I have ever been. What good am I to You right now? My only friends are the Lanes and my roommate." Then the Lord softly pointed out how much worse it was when I had moved to Tennessee. I said, "I'm sorry, Lord. You're right. That was really painful, and You have done so much for me since then. I'm not supposed to worry about where my life is going as You are leading me to where You want me to be." Then I looked at the thought for the week in my journal. *"O Lord, deliver me from having to know why."* God is good at reinforcing what we need to hear.☺

Back in Houston, it was time to put things in motion for the fall programs with registration beginning as the ads made their appearance in the newspapers. I also needed to find a good

helper. One of the ladies I met during the first set of classes
was very interested. I gave her the starting materials to go
through, and then she observed the Thursday night classes at
one mall. That Saturday, I was teaching that same lesson at the
next store, but I had a sore throat and could hardly talk, so
Rachel ended up teaching while I was her helper. She liked it,
even though she had gotten a crash course, and she was good
with the students. She was a very good teacher and dependable,
one factor I needed in this business. We worked through the
programs in the fall "team teaching." One time the store was
having a terrific shoe sale, and I needed a new pair of black
flats, so Rachel took the next set of students. When I came back
before class was over with five shoeboxes, her eyes got big! I
said, "They are all Life Stride and were less than $100 total."
The students were the older girls who got caught up in the
excitement and laughed along with us! I taught the last class as
Rachel went shopping.☺ We got along great.

By the end of October, we were finishing the last of the
programs before the Thanksgiving holiday. I thanked God for
the business that He had blessed since my arrival just over six
months ago, for my roommate, and this special young lady who
was now a good instructor with my business. That part of my
life was going well. But I was still feeling discouragement and
loneliness in my social life; there was very little of that. With
my extroverted personality, that was hard. I went to church
alone and came home alone. Dining out alone was no fun, so I
ended up eating takeouts. The walks in the park or going to the
pool were only for exercise and fresh air. The aerobics at 6:00
a.m. several mornings a week were followed by everyone

getting their days started. Though my apartment was bright and roomy, I was spending more time in it than an extrovert enjoys. I now realized how much my dog Suzie had been a comfort. She even listened when I talked.☺

It was during these past few months when being a 'lady alone' really began to bother me. In 1994, after being released from my marriage, I hadn't been looking for a man. I was glad to be free. My only fear was in starting over at my age and making it. Yes, I was lonely at times, and my heart's desire before I was married was for a godly man and a Christian home. It hadn't been a huge issue for me before as with the few I had dated in Tennessee, I had kept my focus on the Lord: Even as God had said "No" to the last guy I had dated in Knoxville and then again upon arriving in Houston. But I now was fearful and concerned about ending up alone. I didn't want to live for a job. I wasn't feeling plugged into the church and only had a couple of friends here. **I could sense my focus was shifting too much toward feeling the need for a man in my life.** As I began to date again, I was discovering many guys would talk the talk when they knew you loved the Lord, but they didn't walk the walk. It was becoming even clearer to me that unless God put the right man in my life, the chances looked slim!

One day I heard over the Christian radio station that a new singles dating service was interviewing potential members. The first stipulation was that you must be a Christian. It sounded good to me! Needing to drop off paperwork at my printers, I told this precious couple about it. Audrey said, "What could it hurt? You might find that special man or some good friends." Her husband agreed. When Tina got home later that day, I ran it by her. She thought it sounded like a great idea! The day I went for the interview, I felt a little strange never having done anything like this before.

In November I flew into Knoxville, rented a car, and split my time between my two best friends there. Since Mary worked during the week, she got me the two weekends. Ruby had me with her during the week. Mary and I visited precious Suzie. I was thankful God had given her a special loving home. While I was with Mary, we also visited with Karen, my first friend in Knoxville, and Liz, my assistant who now owns the business here. With Ruby, we visited with other ladies, listened to her new tapes, and shared praises, hopes, and all about the dating service. The week of Thanksgiving, I drove to Ohio, first staying with my younger sister and her husband a couple of days, then driving to mothers. I told everyone I stayed with about this Christian dating service, and all thought it would be good just to get me out socially. When I flew into Houston, Tina met me. I told her about the positive comments I had gotten about joining the dating service. She said, "You go for it, Girl!" Within the next few days, I turned in the paperwork for my membership.

December is always a slow month for my business. I already had the programs scheduled in different stores starting in January until after Easter. The paperwork was in for the printers so my time was fairly free. I worked on organizing the business and spent more time with my Lord and in His Word, which is always good. But there was still that nagging feeling of "hopelessness" for things ahead to be different for me. I placed a lot of "hope" on this dating service as I felt God had encouraged me through my friends. When I signed up, they gave me a book called <u>Finding Your Perfect Mate</u>.☺ As I read it, I found that I was already doing quite a few things right: for example, meeting a date first at a restaurant before letting him know where I live and checking him out through someone that I know who knows him, if that's possible.

I decided it was time to check the profiles at the dating service. I went home that afternoon with my chin all the way down to my shoelaces! Talk about being discouraged! There were only about 600 members so far, a large percentage of them being women. The men in my age group were very limited. Also on most of the profiles, the section for writing our testimony was mostly blank! When Tina got home from work that day, I filled her in. She said to just hang in there, as the right one hasn't signed up yet. In my devotions that same day, God was saying, ***"When you are listening to My Voice, the evil one will try with all his might to frustrate you…expect that."***

The next morning I read in James 1:13-21. My devotional went on to say, "We are 'recovering sinners' and just like an alcoholic, always be on guard, as we are just one sin away from falling back into a destructive pattern. Avoid any activity or relationship that will reintroduce us to the sin we hate…the more we expose ourselves to the sin, the less resistant we can be." I knew a couple of my weaknesses had been to rescue and to run ahead of God. They had given me much grief in the past, and I would need to be on guard against them. Well, that didn't put me in a very good frame of mind as I said out loud, "Gee, thanks, Lord, this really made my day!" Then, as I continued in

His Word, I saw that God tests us. He allows Satan to tempt us in order to refine our faith and help us grow in our dependence on Christ. We can resist the temptation to sin by turning to God for strength and choosing to obey His Word. I apologized as I knew His warnings are out of love for us.

The dating services social events got busy. We had a Christmas party, and we began to have Friday night meetings to socialize. I went to look at the new profiles coming in, and found a couple guys that looked interesting, showing their love for the Lord. But they were younger by six and eleven years. One of the ladies began to join me for coffee and pie after the meetings. Paula and I hit it off well. As we shared, we confessed we had gotten our focus on the same guy (who was six years younger than me) and we laughed. She really loved the Lord, and we both knew if we just kept it in God's hands, He would work out the best for each of us. We became the best of friends. For the record, this guy ended up dating and marrying one of the other gals, and I was their maid of honor. A group of about twelve to fourteen of us seemed to "hang out together," mostly to eat and visit. I had a few more dates from my church, only to find more tarnished dimes.

I knew Christmas was going to be quiet as my roommate was going home to see family and her boyfriend. The Lanes and Paula were also to be out of town. Everyone felt badly for me as I was going to be alone on Christmas. I was actually fine with it, looking forward to curling up with a good book. But on Christmas day, my eleven-year younger friend called to see if I was free to go look at the lights. I thought he was just being nice, knowing I was alone, but that was the beginning of our dating. We dated a few months having a good time together, but remained just friends.

1997, What Will This Year Bring

It was January 1st, and after a few hours of sleep, I woke up and just began to reflect over the months since moving to Houston. I knew the Lord had been with me, caring for me by blessing the business. Had there been some rough times? Yes, times of fear in the beginning, then there were times of discouragement. Before joining the dating services, I had gone out with a couple of guys from the church and was very disappointed with their lack of commitment to the Lord. What I was seeing and hearing, even though they were in the church, was that these guys still were making their choices the world's way. When they were not in church, they were no different than any man of the world without any love for God. Now, there were a couple of exceptions, but this was mostly what I was seeing. That was what had perked my interest in the dating service, which was supposed to be only "for Christians." I guess that definition can vary. I now call those who really love the Lord, Believers or Christ's followers.

Tina had planned another trip to visit her boyfriend, soon to be her fiancé. I had met him a couple of times when he visited Tina, and really liked him; they were good together. I was very happy for them, but it made me feel even lonelier. The time came for Tina's trip to Alabama. When it was time for her to return, it was on a cold day in mid-January, and we had gotten

sleet earlier in the day. No one was going anywhere in
Houston. She stayed put a couple more days until we were "de-
iced" and had electricity back on. When she got home, it was
good to have her back as we shared, laughing some and crying
some; just being "females" together.☺ Then she told me that
they were praying for God's guidance on when she was to move
to Alabama. The time was coming when I would be alone
again. I knew my roommate was concerned and prayed for me,
as she wanted to see me with that special someone, like hers,
who loves the Lord and wants to be a team for Jesus.

She felt badly for me when I told her about hearing the
"lady's heels" clicking down the sidewalk each morning, and
again in the late afternoon. I could see this sad looking older
spinster lady from my office window each morning as she left
her apartment for work and hear her as she passed under my
window. Then, when she came home I would hear that same
sound. It was such an eerie sound as I would stop my work and
think about her. Only once had I seen her up close. I was just
getting out of my car as she was getting groceries out of hers. I
spoke, and she just gave me a quick glance and looked away. I
asked if I could help her. She said, "No," as she turned to go up
the walk without a smile. I could feel loneliness and sadness
coming from her. Her eyes seemed to say; "I've been hurt and
have shut myself off from the world. I don't want or need
friends." As I was telling Tina about it, I began to cry while
asking, "Will I end up lonely like her? Is this all I have to look
forward to? Going to work and crawling into my apartment
when I'm done?" These questions haunted my soul…as that
sound echoed loneliness in my ears with each click. Tina tried

to console me by reminding me that God had not forgotten me. He did have a plan for me. When I shared this with Paula, even though she had not heard the clicking of this lady's heels, she said this was a fear of hers, too. Was Satan trying to discourage us?

During those first few months of 1997, there were some highs and some lows. The business was going very well; classes were full and Rachel was a real blessing. I still went out with my eleven-year-younger friend, even threw a surprise birthday party for him with Paula's help. But we were just friends. The dating service had a couple of nice outings; the best being a ski trip to Breckenridge, Colorado. Three of us gals had shared a beautiful condo with a fireplace and a gorgeous view from three big windows in the front room. Seventeen members had gone from the dating service. None of us were dating so just had a good time. We ended each of the four days by eating together at different restaurants and sharing our various dishes.

Back home in Houston, even with these times of enjoyment with the group, Paula and I were beginning to see that within a few months, this group would no longer be. Some had job moves ahead, others had relationships and even a marriage, so most of the group would be going in different directions. I had felt so much hope for finding that special someone through this group when I had joined. Now I was really struggling with it. **Would my life ever be more than working hard and being alone?** I even began to feel maybe God was punishing me for running ahead of Him before, and this life of loneliness may be my punishment. Now, ladies, just who do you think whispered that in my ear? Right! The father of lies, Satan himself, was trying to discourage me. But I still knew in my heart, as I stated earlier in this book, that God was either going to answer that prayer for a godly man and marriage, or He would remove the desire in His timing and show me what He did have for me.

Easter was almost here. I had been very busy since the programs had started the third week in January. I thanked my Heavenly Father, as business had been great! Now I was looking for more helpers for both Rachel and me, but again, the problem was finding ladies willing to work evenings and Saturdays. Tina was having problems at work now, so we were both stressed. She was asking God for direction about when she was to move to Alabama where her fiancé lives. She began to look for a job there. We used one another as sounding boards and prayer partners to encourage each other.

There were fewer activities with the dating service. Paula and I were beginning to feel like new members when we did go. Their staff had changed; they had enlarged their office, adding a library, losing the cozy, friendly feel. We were both struggling with feeling comfortable there. Most of our group were no longer around or going to any of the functions. Paula and I were doing more together, but our dating lives were "the pits." If we did have a date, it was usually just another "tarnished dime." We were quite a pair, as we talked out how we felt. We were a couple of discouraged and lonely ladies, but God already knew we would be and that we would need a good friend to be there for us, so He had put us together. Our first desire was to only date guys who were walking with the Lord, so we used each other to hold us accountable. We tried to encourage one another. When I would date someone who turned out to be a "jerk," and the world is not short of them, Paula would cheer me on to go into the dating service, review new profiles to put in a couple of invites, or I would encourage her to do the same. Then we would console each other when it didn't work out. I'm sure the single ones of you reading this can identify.

About this time, I met a man at church who had gone there several years. He sat next to me in Bible Study class. He seemed like a nice man, and we knew some the same of people. We dated for a few weeks and I began to see some things that bothered me, so I told Paula my concerns. I continued to date him a few more weeks, but he was always picking on other people about things from the past. Then he started on me. When I told Paula some of the things he had said to me, she got upset and said, *"This is not the man you prayed for. He's putting you down to make himself feel better.* **Get rid of him!** *When God puts that special one in your life, he won't drain you, he will lift you up."* I knew she was right. He was another tarnished dime with a lot of head knowledge, but his walk was out-of-step with God. The more time I spent with him, the more I saw his selfishness and how he would justify at different times walking just like the world.

Recently, I was sitting in a plane on the runway during a pouring rain, waiting to fly home to Ohio. The young lady next to me said, "I hope they don't cancel this flight because of the rain." A second or two later the announcement came. A brake had locked up. We were taxiing back and would have about an hour and a half delay, but everyone was to remain on the plane. I looked at the young lady, smiled and said, "If we have a brake problem, I want them to fix it." She laughed and agreed. We introduced ourselves. I had noticed she was reading her Bible, and she had noticed the book by Kay Arthur that I was reviewing. She was thirty, never married, but would like to be.

She wanted to know what the book was about. I gave her a brief summary and told her I was reviewing it for notes on some writing that I was doing. Then I told her about the disappointments of dating in my years of singleness and asked her what she was finding. She had the same disappointments. She nodded saying she could identify as I told her about the "tarnished dimes" chapter to be in this book. The book is to encourage ladies to hang in there, while praying for the right mate, if that is in His plan. If not, for her to wait to see what is His plan. She agreed saying she was doing that, not wanting to settle for less than God's best. She said the singles group at her church was like a family. They helped each other out, fixed dinners together, and were friends, even though there wasn't much dating within the group. I told her that was the way the dating service had been before they had gotten bigger; that core of friends had been good. God's most precious jewels are those special friends He brings into our lives. Sometimes we are so focused on what we're asking God for we can miss the jewels He sends our way. Then I told her about Paula and me in Houston. If we had been so focused on the "date" we were praying for, we would have missed the special friendship God had given us. At that point in our lives, God knew that was what we needed. Before we got off the plane in Atlanta, I passed on to her something a counselor friend had told me to watch for when dating. **"Watch what they do, NOT what**

they say." She laughed while saying that was good advice! I said it was great advice and had worked several times for me, showing me to move on, whether he was a tarnished dime, or even worse, a counterfeit, but that's another chapter.

As I got on the next flight to Ohio, my mind was still reviewing that conversation. Yes, those friends God puts into our lives are precious. I began to think about how much Paula's friendship had meant to me. I remembered one special time after we had met for dinner. She was really down. Nothing in the dating service had worked for her. I had tried to lift her spirit, but knew she was still in a low mode when we parted. I had just gotten home after seeing her and the phone rang. She wanted to tell me what happened after she started for home. She was crying and upset with God, and asking why He hadn't put that someone special in her life yet. Even if it wasn't time for the right one, she had asked for someone to spend time with, going to the movies and out to eat, just as a friend if nothing else. Then she began to laugh, saying it was like God hit her up the side of her head and said, I DID send someone, I sent you Ann! (That's me. I've gone by Ann since I was a child.) While we were both laughing I managed to say, "You weren't specific enough, you didn't say you wanted a male friend." After that, when I would get down and wonder why God had moved me to Texas, Paula would say, "He brought you here for me. He knew I needed a friend like you!" ☺

When God put Paula and I together, He knew how much our hearts' desires were alike: Who better than someone with the same pain of loneliness to encourage the other. We really do need a friend or two like this while we are going through life's disappointing times. Loneliness, disappointment, and a lack of hope are the times when Satan will work hard on us, putting the fear of "what if's" in our minds. If we are not careful to keep our eyes on our Savior and Lord, this is when we may become tarnished dimes, by giving in and stepping back into the world, even if it's only to drag our toes in it. Our Heavenly Father was teaching us to focus so much on what He was in our lives that we would be able to lay our heart's desire at His feet and then let it go only to receive it if it were in His plan for us.

One day while visiting with my printers, Audrey said she had a friend who knew a guy who wanted to meet a Christian lady. Would I be interested in a blind date? She and Carl didn't know him, but this other couple did. I agreed to give him a date. He lived almost two hours away, but he drove into Houston to take me to dinner. By the end of dinner, I knew this was not a match, but our time together was not to end easily. When we got back to my apartment, he walked me to the door and I said goodnight. In a few minutes, there was a knock on the door; his car wouldn't start. Could he jump his car with mine? Neither of us had jumper cables, so we drove my car to a Wal-mart that was open 24 hours to get the jumper cable. It still wouldn't start, so he was going to work on it some thinking he knew what the problem was now. I went back inside but in a few minutes, there was another knock at the door. He needed to call a friend to come and get him, but since it was almost two in the morning and his friend also lived two hours away, could he crash on my sofa and call in the morning? By this time, I just wanted to get some sleep, so I gave him a pillow and sheet and told him he needed to be out in the morning.

At 5:40 I got up to go to Aerobics, tiptoed down the hall past him and out the door. It never crossed my mind until on my drive back home to think about Tina. If she got up before I got home, what would she think? She always headed for the coffee pot first which was just past the living room where he was sound asleep. I opened the door quietly. He was still snoring. Then Tina appeared at the end of the hall, pointing at him and mouthing, "Who is he?" I motioned for her to go into her bathroom. When I told her about the evening, we were in stitches. Then I said I had just thought about "what if" Tina gets up and walks past this stranger in her nightshirt, a man, sleeping on our living room sofa. By this time, we were laughing so hard as she filled me in on her side of the story. I was right on what I had visualized. Tina had already told me she knew I was to write this book, so at one point when she was able to talk, she controlled her laughter long enough to say; now this needs to be in your book! ☺

I included this story to illustrate a couple of points. Although I don't think of this man as being a "tarnished dime," as I felt he was a believer, he was a very new one having very little knowledge from God's Word. Even though he was excited about being a Christian he still thought a lot like the world. At one point that evening I had turned around to see this guy down on one knee checking out my derriere as he said, "I approve." I felt he should have been checking out my spiritual side first! Remember about more mature believers being as unequally yoked with a new believer as a non-believer? This blind date and I were at different levels on most things, which was why I made the point of saying by the end of the evening (to myself) it was time to move on. I included this story as it happened during this time of my journey. My point being, too many times, this is what we are finding in our churches. Are these men praying while waiting to see if God is putting this relationship together? They want a Christian gal, but their mindsets are no different than the guys of the world.

Paula and I had discussed this often. Were our standards too high? No, God's Word is truth, but the world would like us to believe life is different today. A man I had dated actually told me, once a person had been married, but now is single, he thought God would understand. Do you get the drift of what he was saying here? I did! I quickly said I didn't see any place in the Bible where God had changed His mind and added that exception. You gals reading this who are single and really want a godly husband, know God says, "Wait." Wait for God to show the man for you. That man will be one who really loves the Lord and lives by God's standards. If you will put this desire in God's Hand, He will place His love in this man's heart for you if that is Gods best for you. If not, He will give you a real love for what He does have for you.

One day, Paula gave me a picture of a lady sitting on a park bench waiting for the right man. She had waited so long she was now a skeleton. We both laughed about it, but also said we didn't want to waste our time waiting. We wanted to do and be what our Lord wanted now, trusting Him with our future. In that way there wouldn't be wasted years of wanting our desires, but years of following His desires. ***"Let us not grow weary in doing good, for at the proper time "in due*** *season" we will reap a harvest of blessing, if we didn't give up."* (**Galatians 6:9**) I can't tell you how many times Paula and I would encourage each other with that one. We had to admit there had been times when it would have been easy to settle for less than what God wanted for us. But no, we were to wait on God, for His proper time, for His due season.

Have you noticed how many times the Lord pointed out to me to "remember" what He has done in the past for me? How He has protected me, provided for me, led me with His loving hand and loved me with His perfect love. Then He asked me to trust Him with my future. Why is that so hard to do? But it is! If we don't really hang on to Him every day, we are prone to take things back into our hands and take a detour. Often we allow Satan to fill our minds with fear and to listen to his untruths, instead of listening to our Heavenly Father who loves us unconditionally. I read a book a couple of years ago that showed me who I have been like much of the time. The main character is "Much-Afraid." The book is an allegory, called Hinds' Feet on High Places. I really identified with her fears, but also with her heart. *She wanted to be with the great Shepherd as He lovingly taught her to let go of the world, follow Him, give to Him her heart's desire, and to trust Him.* The story goes on to say; *"Only then can He give her His Best."*

5

~

My Dime—Someone Else's Dollar

God had given me the first seven chapter titles about two years prior to His letting me know that it was time to begin writing this book. The other titles I understood immediately, but this one was a little puzzling at first. As I began thinking it through, I realized how important this chapter had been in my journey. I had learned that even though I may meet a very special guy who really loves the Lord, one who has all the qualities I admire he may still not be in God's plan for me. When God has other plans, He will say, "NO." We need to listen, or we both will miss God's best.

Once I began to think about what the Lord wanted you all to see from this chapter, I remembered two examples He had already given me. There has been one since. All three were very different, but all matched this title. My first example of "someone else's dollar" goes back to my life in Tennessee. The second happened during the time I was in Houston. The third example looks to the future after moving from Houston.

My journey for this chapter begins toward the end of May 1997. Paula and I were both in a low mode feeling God had forgotten our heart's desires for a mate. It seemed the odds were not very good that our lives would ever change. As I remembered reading about the Valley of Baca in Psalm 84, I knew God spoke to me then, but He was also speaking to me now. *"No good thing does He withhold from those whose walk is blameless."* (Verse 11) In my application Bible it says, **"God does not promise to give us everything we think is good, but when we obey Him, He will not hold anything back that will help us to serve Him."** Paula and I were afraid the Lord may choose for us to remain single.

In Tennessee the first example for this chapter was introduced into my life. I had really admired this man's heart for the Lord, and we had so much in common. Within a few weeks I knew in my heart God was saying, "No." Later, I had felt God softly whisper, "He is for someone else, he is to be someone else's dollar." Here I was, a year and a half later, and that man in Tennessee was getting ready to marry the other lady. Other than my friend Joel, for whom God had also said "No," there had not been anyone for me. I had prayed for the Lord to help me be faithful in all things and to help me with my unbelief. He was doing His part, but I wasn't there yet. I just wasn't quite ready to let go. I was hanging on to this heart's desire for a godly husband and a Christian marriage, begging God to answer this prayer. It's hard to let go of something we want so badly. After all, God may not have it in His plans for us. That's God's point! My flesh still wanted my way on my desire. My head knew God's way would ALWAYS be best, but in my heart I wanted this too much. I didn't trust the Lord with every area in my life yet. Now, I will add this. If we pray for our Lord to remove the desire if it is not in His plan for us, He will. I could not see it then, but I am amazed at God's patience with me. I look back now over the years I put myself through a lot of agony unnecessarily by not fully surrendering that area of my life sooner.

It was Memorial Day weekend. Paula had invited me to go to her church picnic. She attended a small country church where all were like family. Thinking we might click, Paula introduced me to one of the guys who sang in the praise and worship service with her. She filled me in about this guy's love for the Lord. He was good-looking and friendly. When Paula asked what I thought, I said, "I can see the two of you together. He's your type, and I know you like him." At that point, however, Paula had a crush on another guy in her church. I also met him but thought she fit better with the one she had introduced to me.

Life is funny sometimes when we look back and see what God already knew was going to happen. During that coming summer, Paula did end up dating the other guy she had a crush on a couple of times, then agonized over why it wasn't working out. I finally told her that this guy couldn't be the right one as just thinking about the relationship was constantly draining her. Now I was feeling empty from not having a special someone in my life and sensing a loss of hope as well. I hadn't yet figured out that if my focus were where it should have been, I would have had peace just knowing that my future was in God's hands, instead of wringing mine! To make a long story short, Paula and the guy she had tried to put with me have been happily married for over four years. It was neat to see in God's timing how He put them together.☺ Even though Dan had no idea that we were sizing him up on that Saturday, God knew the ending. Dan would have been a dime for me, because he was to be my friend's dollar.

The week after Memorial Day, Tina began her move to Alabama. I was glad I was flying to Knoxville for a short visit before driving to Ohio to see my family. Tina took me to the airport, but would be gone when I returned. She and her fiancé would be back for the final move the week after my return home. We would not be "roomies" anymore.☹

My summer schedule had changed. Two of the department stores where I was to have had programs were in the middle of construction, so thought it best to do the programs after the remodeling was completed. I quickly submitted a new schedule, moving one of the programs I had booked later back to summer. The new schedule was OK'd and we were ready to go with the first ad. This had been a real scare for me. It was the first time since moving to Houston that any of my classes had been canceled.

I began to realize if I were going to stay here and continue to work this business, I would need to diversify. Schools, junior colleges, and a dance group had asked me to do classes with their students, but I was so busy I had not committed to working with them. I began to rethink my options and contacted some of these people. I added the program for the dance group and one class at a school. I also talked with one of the junior colleges, but our schedules wouldn't line up.

I was back to the same dilemma. I needed more helpers to expand the business. I would hire someone who would work a time or two and then she would decide it interfered with her schedule. One of the ladies from my cell group ministry was a good helper when I needed her but only at the locations near her home. Since she had a day job, she couldn't come until the second-class session. I used her more on the last night of the program to help with the graduation and fashion shows. Finally, I just said, "Lord, if you want me to expand, you will need to bring the teachers and helpers to me as you have in the past."

Paula and I continued getting out together. I found if we met for lunch at least once a week it got me out of my apartment during the day. I still met Dee for lunch about once during the week and was occasionally invited to their home to do something with their family. That was about it for my social life. I did have a few dates between the dating service and church, but work was still the main part of my life. I was adjusting to life alone.

In mid August I received a phone call from an Orlando friend. Sharie and I had been good friends since the late 1980's. She told me about a man who had just committed suicide from our Bible study class. His wife, Sharie, and I had all been friends. He had embezzled money from his business and had gotten in too deep. I was numb, between feeling sorry for his wife and not being able to grasp how he could take his own life. What was Sharie saying about the money?

He had been a financial advisor who invested people's money. Sharie said that it looked like his investors had lost everything. Now I focused on every word. I replied, "Sharie, I invested with him, ALL of my IRA's and most of my savings from Tennessee, which was a large part of my retirement." Sharie hadn't known I had trusted him to invest my money. She had just called to let me know the sad news since I knew him and his wife. I was stunned! I would have trusted him with the shirt on my back! How could this be as it was a secure company he worked for, or so we had all been led to believe? Nothing was clear right now, but it looked like he had done a good "scam job." Sharie said, if she and Roy had had some extra money to invest, they would have trusted him, too. I knew she was hurting for me as she and Roy knew better than a lot of my friends how much I had struggled in Tennessee, sometimes just having enough to get by. I had invested that money so I wouldn't be tempted to use it, so it would be there for me in later years when I would no longer be able to work.

Talk about being jolted right down to my shoes and socks! All I could do was fall to my knees and sob, "Why, Lord, why did this happen?" I had been working so hard, and God had been blessing me with enough income to save and add to what I had. My teacher's retirement would not be much, so I knew what I needed to save, and now, I was so far behind my goal.

How many more years could I work like this? I'm over 50 years old now!

When I told Paula and Dee the next day, they felt badly for me. I just wanted to "give up," go to bed and never get up. What was the use? I have always had to work hard and still have had more than my share of struggles. I knew in my mind that Satan was trying to discourage me, but I also knew that my Lord had allowed it, and I was upset with that. What I was feeling now was anger! While I had been working hard to bring it in the front door, it had been sucked out the back door. I had always given God the glory for how well the program was being received. So, why?

Yes, I was discouraged. Satan was winning at this point, wasn't he? I've since learned that it is OK to tell God when you are upset with Him as long as you don't walk away from Him. But it had shaken my confidence in God's care. I hadn't stopped knowing I should trust the Lord, but on reflecting, I did take a step back at that point, putting just a little distance between us. My Lord and Savior knew what I had been through. He knew all of the struggles, and He knew I wanted to be and do what He wanted. This seemed to be a cruel blow I hadn't deserved.

Have any of you ever felt like that? I'm sharing this because I want you to know how easily we can listen to Satan's lies when we are discouraged, disappointed and, yes, angry, angry with God for allowing something like this to happen. We are most apt to feel this way when we are already tired, lonely, fearful, or discouraged. Those were my feelings. However, this is when we need to hang on to our Lord Jesus the tightest.

Looking back, it is easy to see how Satan was working hard to discourage me.

It was now the end of August. My aerobics instructor knew I was discouraged about my dating life, or lack thereof, and about the direction for my business. She had been where I am now and understood what I was going through. I also knew she had prayed for that special someone to come along for me. One morning she gave me a big smile and said, *"I've been thinking about what you need. I think God is going to bring a man into your life that has been widowed after many years of marriage. He will have God's love in his heart for you and will cherish your heart as you have prayed for."* I laughed while saying, "I'm ready." But God knew that I wasn't, not yet. Was this prophetic? Only God knew what was ahead for this lady!

Fall came and went as I was working hard with all the programs I had scheduled. My assistant was doing great, but I couldn't find a helper for her or myself who lasted. Paula moved her mother to a small apartment close to where she lived, so her life was busy. We still went out occasionally for lunches, but talked more by phone. I began helping more at the pregnancy center where I had volunteered for the past six months.

I was spending more time in prayer and in God's Word. My Lord always spoke to me through His Word and the devotional, but one morning, He spoke to me through the thought for the day *"fire refines gold, adversity refines man."* The Scripture reading was 1Peter 1:3-9. I sat for a while just thinking about it, then spoke out loud saying, "I've had enough adversity, Lord, don't You think?" There was silence. Then I felt like laughing as I said, "I really didn't think you would give me an answer on that one." There were times when I could almost feel His hand on my shoulder to encourage me; this was one of those times. Then on a Sunday morning in mid-October, my Bible study was from Genesis 10 & 11. The main thrust was that **"God has a plan for our lives, even when we are like the three-year-old, trying to live by his own agenda."** I thought about that later, looked up and said, "OK, Lord, what is your plan for me? I know that You knew before I was born, the detours and mistakes I would make and where I would be at this moment in time. I know that Your Plan is that my life will bring You glory; I desire that, too, Lord."

It is now January of 1998. The holidays had come and gone so quickly. I had gone home to see my family in Ohio for Thanksgiving, and spent Christmas break in Orlando with my son and friends. My winter and spring line-ups for the business were all completed before the holidays. I interviewed a young lady to be a helper for Rachel. She started with me the last week of January, so I could get her trained at the classes that I was doing. My assistant had needed to work more at the hospital in January and February, so that meant I had no relief. I did hire a couple more helpers, but they didn't last. I was working all of the hours and was exhausted! Just reading my journal now from that time in my life makes me tired!!

Then on February 16th on a Monday night, the new lady I was training and I were to complete the last class for that program, finishing with their graduation and fashion show. The day had been rainy and nasty, but by the time I was driving to the mall to start the classes, the rain had stopped and it was beautiful. My helper arrived about an hour later due to her day job. She said it looked bad outside again and had begun to rain just as she got inside the mall. We completed the class with the 1st-3rd graders and had taken the attendance for the 4th-6th graders. They were settled in their seats when it happened. I heard what sounded like a long, long roll of thunder. I looked at my helper. Her eyes were as big as saucers as she stared past our doorway. I turned to look. The ceiling tiles were blowing all over in the area next to our room. A tornado had hit the end of the mall, which was the front of the store. The only thing between my back and the brick wall (that was now gone,) was an <u>open</u> stair well and an interior plasterboard wall that I was standing in front of. We were on the second floor. I got the class together and with my helper and a set of scared parents who had run back to see their daughter, we got the class down the escalator, which of course, was no longer working, and into the arms of their parents. I was glad for the training I had as a teacher. When my helper and I got to our cars, they were fine, but many others had not been so fortunate.

When I got home, I called Paula to see if she was all right since she lived fairly close. She was, so I told her about my experience. Having just seen the movie "The Titanic," I said I felt like I had been on it as I had waded in water and merchandise above my ankles, wearing my favorite heels. The sprinkler systems had broken. There was no reason why the ceiling tile in our room wasn't blowing out of the frame as it was just outside the doorway and all over the rest of the second floor. The walls that stood around us should have been blown down. In our room there was no movement of the floor others described. **There has never been any doubt in my mind, heart or soul that God's arms of protection were around us that day.**

March and April were extremely busy months with the business. My assistant was back on the regular schedule. I had overlapped classes which meant there were times when she would be doing classes one place and I another. Business was good, but I wanted to move back to where I felt was home, Orlando. I thought about selling the business, asking my assistant if she was interested. She was, but she and her husband didn't have the money. I couldn't afford to give the business away with my finances the way they were! I had too many hours of hard work and tears invested and still needed the income for my future. It wasn't the territory that was worth any more, but the business that my Heavenly Father had enabled me to build was worth a lot more. So, I figured out a plan where I would pay my assistant more for the classes she did. I would fly over every three months, and stay a month doing the extra classes, earning all of that income myself. While I was there, I would make sure my assistant had the materials she needed until I returned. I would get an 800 number, and do all of the business planning and the class registrations. That was somewhat like I had done when I ran the program in North Carolina while I lived in Knoxville. This time instead of driving between the two, I would need to fly. My assistant agreed to the plan and the pay.

When I told Paula about wanting to move, she understood. She was so busy with her mother and her daughters, and I with the business that neither of us felt we had a life. I had been down emotionally ever since I lost so much of my savings in the fall. I felt if I moved back to where my son and many of my friends lived, plus the church that I loved, at least, the quality of life would be better. The move was set for May. If I had known what that next year or so would hold, I may have crawled in bed and stayed there!

Before leaving this chapter I must tell you all about the third man in my life who was someone else's dollar. Remember, I said at the beginning of this chapter that there was one in the future to be included under the title of this chapter. It was about two years after I moved back to Orlando that I met this man at a sales meeting for a business we were both considering. As we got to know one another through a few casual dates, mostly double dates with friends, and time on the phone, I knew there was a genuine "like" on both sides. One of the first things he had shared with me was his testimony. He had a real love for Jesus. That was good! Also, we both had a love for playing tennis. One night he told me about his former wife, and how she had some problems. He felt he needed to be there for her and get her some help. I had prayed about our friendship, as I knew I was always "guarding my heart" around him. I asked my friends to pray about it. They and my younger sister gave me the same answer that I had felt, for I had prayed for a man who would cherish my heart; but he couldn't, for his heart still belonged to another. We remained friends, sending an occasional email message or talking on the phone. Once in a while, we would meet for a cup of coffee to catch-up on our lives and to encourage each other. It was a good friendship.

In this chapter I have given three examples for "someone

else's dollar." All were quite different. Both the first and third had feelings of "genuine like" involved on both sides and in both examples, we had dated before I knew in my heart the Lord was saying, *"No, this one belongs to another."* In the second example, although Dan seemed to have what I had desired in a man, I sensed God saying, "No, he's not for you; without the first date. Then the feeling that this man and my friend Paula would be good together." I had told Paula at that time I felt she and Dan were for each other, but I had not realized how strongly I felt that until over eighteen months later when she called, all excited, to tell me about their dating. I got excited, too, saying, "I knew it, I knew God was putting that in my mind! I felt you two should be together!" ☺

In the first paragraph of this chapter I had written that I realized how important this chapter had been on my journey. What I was seeing was, even while we are close to our Lord, someone else's dollars are much harder to see. The dimes of the world are fairly easy to spot, as you should see a difference in how they think and behave. Those who are shiny dimes have just begun their journey with their Lord, or are not as mature in their faith; these differences will show up as we spend just a little time with them. But those who are a dime, although a very special dime to us, because it's God's plan that they be with someone else, are more difficult to see. We must be praying for our Lord to show us if being teamed with this person is God's plan for us. When we are looking to our Lord and Savior for His answer, He will give it. If you recall, on that first example, the Lord didn't give me a reason, He just said, "No." Later the Lord said this man was for someone else, but not until I had obeyed Him.

Of course in all of this, the main thought is if we keep our focus on Jesus, He will not let us wander from His path.

Now, let's continue on together as I move from Houston, back to Orlando in chapter 6. Only God knew what lay ahead for me....

6

~

The "Counterfeit"

All that glitters is not gold. *As we start this chapter, it is important to define the main point of this leg of my journey. Webster's dictionary defines a <u>counterfeit</u> as being " forged, false, made to imitate something else with a view to defraud." What is a <u>deceiver</u>? "One who misleads; one who leads to err, a fraud as a counterfeit." And lastly, what is <u>deception</u>? "It is the act or practice of deceiving; an illusion, or impostor." These are the definitions given by the world.*

What do you think God's Word says it means? Surprisingly, very much the same, only in the Bible it speaks of the deceiver and the deception, which is the counterfeit. The first time God's Word tells us about deception and the deceiver is in Genesis 3:6 when Satan started it all with Eve. It has been going on ever since with Satan working through people to work his deception on others.

With all of that said, it's time to get back to this journey. As we finished chapter five, it was the first of May in 1998, almost two years to the day since I moved from Tennessee to Texas. Was I ready for another move? I was so happy to be going back to Florida where I felt at home. As for the business, I had the programs lined up for my assistant in Houston to teach all through the summer and fall up to the holidays. In the fall, I would be flying back to do the extra classes while getting the preparations made for the next set of programs to begin after the first of the year. Tearful good-bys were said with my friends at the pregnancy center, and the couple who had been my printers for the business, but the hardest were leaving Paula, and Dee and Craig.

The day came for the move. Packing was done and sent on ahead. I had planned to drive, enjoying the ride, taking some extra time in the Panhandle of Florida, (since I had never been there.) It was beautiful! I rolled down the windows letting the wind blow through my hair as I enjoyed the scenic white sandy beaches while listening to some beautiful piano music. I even stopped a couple of times to take a walk and watch the seagulls soar while taking pictures. Yah!! I was back home, back in Florida! Thank you, Lord!! I said that over and over as I was driving.

Now as I look back I realize my Lord and Savior was NOT

as happy about the move as I was, nor with me, for I was running ahead of Him. I was doing what seemed like the right thing to me. I had slipped into the driver's seat, taking back the control of my life, seeing the future the way I wanted it to be. I had asked my Lord and Savior about the move, but I hadn't stayed quiet before Him to listen for His answer. Although I did see a move to Florida was in God's plan, I excitedly ran ahead shouting, "Yes, Lord, let's go!!" Have you ever done that? It's so easy, when the journey ahead is taking you where you want to go, to just jump up and start moving. This was unlike when I knew the Lord was leading me to Tennessee. I had wanted to move to Florida then, remember? I had asked the Lord to clear the path ahead if this was truly His plan. It was the same when I was moving to Texas. But this time, I had not asked the Lord to clear the path ahead to know this was His leading. **I had felt that I was going to paradise; but the crafty snake with his deception awaited me there.**

Once I was settled into a rented condo, I got the business things in place. First, I needed my 800#, and then I got my computer, printer and office area ready to go. That summer went well with going back to the church I loved, being close to my son and many of my friends. I really liked the area. It was a different location from where I lived between 1985 and 1992, but the road access was good with very convenient shopping. The condo was in a gated community with a lake to the back, two pools, a tennis court, plus the clubhouse that I appreciated using for parties. The air smelled fresh with many trees to shade the walkways. I felt safe as the gates kept the traffic down, and it was so quiet: A perfect place to talk with my Lord as I walked, which is something I have enjoyed doing for years. I especially loved the evenings when I could take in the beautiful Florida sunsets over the lake, absolutely breathtaking! Isn't God good to give us such beauty to enjoy while we are here?

Fall arrived quickly and with it the need to fly to Houston to work on the business. Class registrations were completed for the programs that would be going on while I was there. I also needed to spend more time in the department stores with the managers. In that region, managers and their assistants were moving around so fast my chart was beginning to look like a pincushion with lots of red detour lines! They were also bringing in new people who didn't know the value of my program to their store. It was my job to keep them informed so my "special event" didn't get cancelled. It was much harder than I had thought to stay on top of the business with so many miles between. I rented an efficiency for three weeks to run the business. Since I was feeling so stressed, I needed a few get-away times with friends. I had even made an appointment with my hairdresser for one of her great haircuts while in Houston. Now, that's important to us ladies. Right? Just before leaving, I met with my assistant for a final check on the schedule to begin after the holidays and to go through to summer, making sure that we were on the same page.

On the flight home, I knew I would rather move on to something else less wearing, and sell the business, but how? I would need to sell it for close to what it was worth for the income to get me started in Florida until I could find some other income. Although I knew the Lord had cleared the way for the

128

business to succeed, I had worked hard for two years, building the business from seven store locations to sixteen. Most of them were hosting my program two or three times per year. God had opened the doors but I was to do the plowing. To accomplish this I worked many sixteen-hour days. Early on I learned that God expects us to put feet to our prayers and my feet were very tired!

I was feeling a great deal of stress over the decision about whether I should sell the Houston territory. It had made a good living while I was there. But now, between the added expenses of running it from so many miles away, plus the inability to maintain the PR with the department stores and the personal contact with the parents of my students, it had become quite stressful. At the same time I was also concerned as I had been looking for a way to make my living in Florida, but with no results. **It was about this time I realized I had run ahead of God to get here, taking back the control. Had He abandoned me?** I could not see His direction or feel His presence as before. Was He stepping back and leaving me on my own? I felt like a child who has run ahead of his parents to do what he wants, only to look back and not see them anywhere now! The fear grips him, as he wants more than anything to see his father. That was the way I felt. I wanted to hear my Heavenly Father's voice comforting me, but there was silence.

The holidays came and the first of the year 1999 was here so quickly. I had driven home for Thanksgiving and stayed in Orlando for Christmas. Now I was planning my business trip back to Houston the first of February. I was also contacting some business brokers there to check out my options. Paula and

I were looking forward to some extra time together. We were both struggling, feeling we had no life other than our responsibilities. We needed the time to lift each other up while doing something special together. We took a two-day trip to San Antonio and enjoyed the river walk.

While I was in Houston I did a couple of extra programs by myself along with helping my assistant with a couple of hers. Business was doing well. I also worked on scheduling more programs, completing the schedule through next fall, which would bring us around to the holidays again. Then the day came for the appointment with one of the business brokers. When Paula got home from work that afternoon, we went out to dinner together. I could hardly wait to tell her about the meeting; I wanted to see her expression. "Paula," I said, "I almost fell out of my chair when this guy told me what my business is worth!" I had invested many hours building up my business for almost three years. I also knew God had blessed it. But when I was told the worth of my business, I stated, "There is no way I would ever get that amount." The gentleman agreed, and came back with a figure I would more likely be paid. This still blew my mind until he explained by comparing my business to another. The example he gave was a catering service. He asked, "Which would you rather own: the new business or the one that had been worked and has customers in place?" Of course, I would rather buy a catering service that already had a good customer base or clientele in place. That was what he was showing me that I had to offer as well.

My mind was spinning! Was this what I should do? I had no other sort of income at this point. But with my need to fly to

Houston twelve to sixteen weeks a year, what job would work with that? I was sure it would be smarter to sell the business and start over again in something else, but what? Selling would give me a nice down payment for a condo but where would the income be to live on? The business the Lord had blessed me with was in Houston, but how could I go back now? From this distance, I felt even more like the juggler in the circus who needs to keep all of the plates spinning at the same time, only now, I was not close enough to see when some of plates begin to wobble. I asked my friends to pray for God to show me His leading so I would make the right decision. I really needed to hear my Heavenly Father's voice. **Why was He silent?**

To give you the answer to that prayer, God gave me a buyer on my next trip to Houston at the end of April. It was for about half what the business broker had told me I should get, but then, there was no commission to pay. Since the buyer came to me through an unusual set of circumstances, I felt strongly that this was God's answer for me. The deal was completed by the end of May.

By mid August, I had bought my own condo. I was ecstatic when it had opened up in the area where I had been living, enjoying my walks, the pool, tennis courts and, of course, the sunsets over the lake. From the first time I walked into that condo, it felt like home.☺ All the things I had asked God for were there: a sunroom type enclosed porch, split plan for my office and bedroom, an extra area for a den, plus a garage for my car. Again, I saw God's grace, love and provision. The Lord was just blowing my mind! He often gives us more than we even ask for. The condo was on a beautifully landscaped big, corner lot. My little house even had a couple of skylights for extra light or to hear the pitter pat of rain, both of which I loved. What a bonus!! And it was so peaceful and quiet. **But the biggest bonus was that I could feel the Lord's presence again.**

The Lord had given me my first real home since my divorce in 1994. I am a nester, and how I enjoyed the holidays that year in my little house. Looking back, I know the Lord had wanted this home to be a special home, one where I would grow closer to Him than ever before. It would be where I was to finally give to Him "my heart's desire for a godly husband" as a sacrifice and to let Him truly be the Lord of "all" my life. While living in my little home, I could always feel the Lord's presence; it was "our home," it really was!

It was the spring of 2000 and I had been back in Orlando for almost two years. But now I need to reflect back over those two years to show you what else was going on in my life. All of us have been fooled at one time or another by those who aren't who they would like us to believe they are, perhaps more often than we would like to admit. Sometimes we are gullible because it looks or sounds so good; something we desire, so we don't want to see it as a lie. When I was going through the shock of losing so much of my savings, how easily Satan had discouraged and weakened me. I had dated several men, all-claiming to have a real relationship with the Lord. However, it was during these two years I had gotten involved in a counterfeit relationship. What I found was that there are times when the line between "real" and "counterfeit" is very blurred and hard to see. That's the way Satan wants it to look, and we may find ourselves questioning what we know to be true, rather than checking whether their lives are true.

I can see now how Satan had been really busy as he brought this man into my life. If you recall in chapter five, I knew in my mind Satan was trying to discourage me when I had lost so much of my retirement money. What I didn't know was he was soon going to toss me the bait, hoping to set the hook. But the Lord was beside me, sometimes being silent, but not allowing me to be pulled under.

My mind drifts back to the time when my counselor friend told me, ***"Before you begin a relationship, remember NOT to listen to what he says, but to watch what he does. This is the way to know who he really is."*** Since that time, I had followed this advice. It had proven a wise step to take. But as I look back at this counterfeit relationship that formed after my return to Florida, I realize I had not done that. On the surface, what the man wanted me to see looked good. He was clever with his words. He was telling me exactly what I wanted to hear and showing me exactly what I wanted to see. It was only when I got close enough to see that his walk wasn't matching his talk that I knew this was not where I was to be.

Real deception is ugly. It is full of lies to bring about the selfish end that the deceiver wants. Once he told his lies it was as if they then became truth to him. I had to deal with the fact that this whole relationship with this man wasn't real since it was all based on lies. Then, I needed to deal with the hurt and anger that I had from allowing myself to be so deceived. After meeting this guy, one of my discerning friends said it best: *"The saddest part was that in trying so hard to delude others, he had in turn deluded himself the most. He wouldn't know truth if it hit him in the face!"* What hurt me the most was in seeing how this man used God and the church for his deception.

How could I have done this! After listening to the Lord through these years, following His lead: whether it was to move, end a relationship, or help in the business, only to mess up now. I had run ahead of God and allowed myself to be taken in by a deceiver. I was so discouraged. Had I blown my testimony? Was this the reason there was now silence? Was the Lord giving up on me? "No," our Lord isn't like that. He was silent long enough for me to realize the mess I was in, and that it had occurred when I had taken my eyes off Him while running ahead, taking my own path. My heart was aching!

I needed to take an honest look at me. How had I allowed myself to be fooled after years of being so careful? What had I done! I woke up one day and realized I had been deceived again. I didn't need to look long, nor very far back in my journey to see where I had taken the detour of "self-control." **I had allowed the "fear" to creep back in while listening to Satan as he whispered;** *"Is this how God is taking care of you? With this money for your retirement gone, what is going to happen to you?"* It was now clear; Satan had used fear trying to defeat me: fear of being alone, fear of failing, fear of not having a man, and fear of not having the income to survive. That had been my weak area. In my head, I knew my God was bigger than my circumstances, and I certainly knew how the Lord had shown me His care, His love and His grace over the past years. But in my heart, my faith had faltered, and I had begun to move ahead unsteadily and with uncertainty. I hadn't fallen, but I was doing some stumbling, causing me to look down at the path before me instead of looking up, trusting the Lord to lead. I feel sure now this is where I am supposed to be, but I did run ahead of God in getting here. My move to Orlando was not in God's timing, but mine.

I repented to my Lord for my sin and asked Him to give me the faith that I needed to trust Him totally for whatever was in my journey ahead: to take any fears away keeping my focus on Him, not the path before me. The Lord knew I was now ready to walk with Him again, so He took my hand. I felt His presence as the Lord reminded me He would not abandon me. I also knew if I would keep my hand in His, He would lead me to His best.

Before moving into chapter 7, a real praise chapter called "The Dollar—God," I would like to close this one with a thought written in my devotional. *"Those who wait on the Lord will never be disappointed."* When we're hurting or in distress over sin, we can look up and wait with anticipation. The Lord will come! Whether through a promise directly from His Word, the wise counsel from a friend, or the quiet witness of the Holy Spirit. **He will meet our need----as certainly as morning light always breaks through the darkness of night.**

7

~

The Dollar-God

It is now late spring in the year 2000. One morning as I was flipping through my Bible, a piece of paper fell out. It was something I had written shortly after moving into my little home early in September of last year (from __My Utmost for His Highest__.) Reading it, tears filled my eyes as I reflected on my life just this past year. I think sharing it with you at this time is the best way to begin this new chapter of my journey.

"God takes you through a way that you temporarily do not understand. And it is ONLY by going through the spiritual confusion that you will come to understand; What God wants for you."

I was thankful that it was a morning when I had time to just sit with the Lord and to look up some of the verses He had given me from His Word over this past decade and to talk with Him about them. The minutes melted into hours as I could feel my Lord's love wash over me. I also sensed His encouragement to step out into the days and years ahead, knowing that He would be with me. He had a plan for my life. My job was to keep my focus on the Lord and to trust my future to Him. I simply needed to wait, watching for His leading in anticipation and with expectancy. A line from a chorus kept going through my mind. *"My life is in You, Lord. My Hope is in You, Lord."* That is the line that I still hear most often in my quiet times with Him.

I knew the Lord wanted this little house to be a special home, one where I would grow even closer to Him. It was here where I truly came to trust Him "totally" with my future. Always before there was still fear of the "what if's." When things weren't going well, I would begin to look for a solution, just in case my Heavenly Father was pre-occupied.☺ Sounds so silly now, but when we are in the middle of a crisis, we often panic and think we need to start swimming to the closest floating object so we won't drown. What I had come to realize was that by the time I had reached that object, I would see it was not what the Lord had for me. The lesson is, if we will just wait for His leading, we will never drown! Plus, we won't be all worn out from thrashing around "needlessly." God's answers are never too early, but neither are they ever too late, and He does take care of the "what if's."

In Matthew 6:25- 34, Jesus says, "Do not worry." There

are several good reasons. It damages our health, consumes our thoughts, disrupts our productivity, negatively affects how we treat others, and primarily reduces our ability to trust God. Satan loves all of these, as they will "side-line" us. Something I read years ago has helped me to know if I have slipped back into worry. *"The difference between worry and genuine concern is that worry immobilizes, but concern moves to action."* In these verses, Jesus also tells us to "**seek first His kingdom**" which means, we are to turn to God FIRST for help and to fill our thoughts with His desires, not ours, then serve and obey our Lord in everything.

Worriers are consumed by fear and find it difficult to trust God. My inability to give God the one area in my life I had agonized over for years was due to my lack of faith and fear it may not turn out my way. But, of course, I wanted His blessing over it. Well, Hello! The Lord was showing me that **I needed to totally let go, so that He could work out His best for me, AND so I would accept His plan with joy in my heart.** Most of our worries and fears are needless, as they never happen anyway. I ran across a word definition that may help you to remember the futility of this kind of fear. **F (false), E (evidence), A (appearing), R (real).** Now, don't let worries about tomorrow affect your relationship with God today.

During the spring that first year in my little home, the Lord had shown me so clearly that *He is all I need now, or in my future.* I finally yielded to Jesus my heart's desire for a godly man to share my life with. I felt lighter in my spirit, as I had asked Jesus to be the center of my life and no longer felt the need for a man. Once I had yielded my desire as a sacrifice to the Lord, I found I was content, being with just Him. He was all I needed. It no longer mattered if God's plan for me was to remain single the rest of my life; only that I would somehow bring the Lord glory. The old heart's desire was replaced by just wanting to be a vessel for the Lord to work through to reach others. My Dollar—God, whom I have trusted for His healing of the past, and His guidance in the present, I now trust totally with my future.

Jesus, our Lord and Savior, has freed us to be all we are to be. He wants to transform past pain into the energy or fuel for future achievement. God can take the pain and sins of our past, and use them for His glory. But, He can't work out His plan until we open our hands, releasing all we have to Him. Only then, can He fill our hands to overflowing.

The Lord began to teach me about the three most important relationships in our lives: with ourselves, with our man, and with God. (And if there is no man, He shows us that He, Jesus, will fill that void perfectly.)

Now about that relationship with ourselves, too often we ladies become a martyr for any cause but our own. We invest our lives into something or someone that is not worthy. Then we get down on ourselves, thinking we can't shine for Jesus. Our Lord wants us to accept ourselves as we see who we are, forgiven and loved by Him since we asked for His forgiveness. We must get beyond the guilt and disappointments of our past to seeing who we are now—His perfect child. Even though we will never be perfect this side of heaven, this is how God sees us and we need to grow toward that end. Satan wants us to live in defeat so our Lord can't use us. **Our heads need to be lifted**

up to see His victories, not with our eyes cast down in defeat.
During the time I lived in my little home, I took more bubble
baths, listened to music I enjoyed, and spent time with my lady
friends, just enjoying life. Yes, I still dated some, but as the
months rolled by, I was seeing that it was now very easy for me
to let go or not begin any dating relationship when I sensed it
was not what God had for me. I felt real joy and peace in
knowing I was just fine now. I was not alone for I had chosen
my Dollar—God: no more of the world's dimes for me! And
the Lord had promised to never leave me, but to be there for me,
leading, caring, and loving. While we are single, we need to
spend that time finding wholeness and learning the art of being
happy alone.

I was looking forward with anticipation, and even
excitement, to seeing HIS plan unfold! Wow, that was the
difference. Looking back, there were many times I thought I
had given this desire of mine to God, only to discover that I was
still hanging on to it. I always had this "dread" in my heart and
in the pit of my stomach that it may be the Lord's desire to use
me "alone" for the rest of my life. I remember a pastor friend in
Houston telling me about a group of ladies doing ministries in
his church who had taken an oath to remain single to be freer
for the Lord to use them. He thought maybe this was a group I
might be interested in joining. I politely said that God had not
taken away that desire yet, nor told me that His plan was for me
to remain single. I was not comfortable with that answer.
Inside my head I was screaming, "NO, I do not want to end up
single and alone." Of course, being single does not make one
alone. I had thought that way because my focus had been too

much on my heart's desire. There was nothing wrong with that desire except my unwillingness to totally give it to God. I was not ready to give up on the hope that someday God might put that special man into my life. Can you see where I was? I was not willing to let God have that part of my life. I was always looking for one who might be the answer from Him. Instead of letting God take care of it, I was trying to do it for Him. I had been busy looking under every rock, or as a dating book suggested, leaving no stone unturned, looking for that special mate.

Although I would not continue dating a guy once I knew he was not the Lord's choice for me, there was a time or two when I had continued to date a guy for a short while beyond when I knew he was not God's answer, simply because I didn't want to be alone. But I always knew in my head and in my heart that I did not want to take any of these detours, wanting to stay on the path where the Lord was leading me. That is, until I ran ahead of God to move back to Florida. Then, He allowed me to be deceived by a counterfeit for a time. And when I was honest with myself, I knew that I had seen what I had wanted to see. For that short time, I had chosen to believe a lie that Satan had whispered in my ear before: fear of being alone. **But NOW that spirit of fear was gone, and this new feeling of freedom felt so good!** Why hadn't I let go sooner? What was I thinking? When I gave my life to Jesus, it was no longer mine, but His! Whatever He has ahead for me will be His best. I knew that years ago, but just could not totally let go of that last area. **I lamented over the time and energy I had spent dwelling on my heart's desire.** Now I rest in my Heavenly

141

Father's arms, asking Him to not let me waste any more time or energy. Instead my desire is to use my time ahead for His glory.

This first year in my little home had been a time for reflection. Why had this one area been so hard for me to yield to my Heavenly Father? As I thought back over my life, I soon realized that when my father passed away while I was only three years old, it had left me with a "lonely spot." You see, my dad had enjoyed carrying me around, putting me on his shoulders, and holding me on his lap as he read to my sister and me while mother fixed a meal. And when he was too sick to carry me he would sit and cuddle me. I remember that whole last year before we lost him. I missed that love through the years that followed. Since my mother needed to go back to work, we soon moved in with grandmother, so she could help in our care. We had a good home in this house filled with just women, my grandmother, my mother, one of her sisters, and my sister, but I missed my father. My Heavenly Father has shown me that He was there for me all that time.

Remember that last line in my poem *"Only God Knows What Lies Ahead?"* I was to know that I could trust Him more than an earthly father. Yes, my father was now with Him in heaven, but my Heavenly Father wanted me to know that He was there, loving me more than I can even imagine. He would carry me when I was tired and comfort me when I hurt.

Mother remarried six years later. I've been told since then that it takes at least seven years to "blend a family." I can see how true that is for we are more like a real family now that we are grown. My stepfather was a good man and very even-tempered, much like I remember my own father as being. When he and my mother married, he had three children of his own. My younger sister is really my stepsister, but we are closer than most real sisters. We are only six months apart in age. We were in the same class, shared many of the same friends and interests, and have turned out to be best friends as well as sisters. My stepfather had asked my mother to quit her job, as we kids needed one of them at home. This meant money was tight. Since my older sister and I received a small monthly check after our dad had passed away, we were told that we would need to pay for our own expenses from that income: schoolbooks, lunches, clothes, life insurance and whatever. As I look back, I became independent at an early age, as I have budgeted since I was ten years old.

I can see now how that made it easy for me to take care of many things in a marriage that were not my responsibility. But that is behind me now as the Lord has been working with me, teaching me to lean on Him. I've needed to learn the huge difference between being so independent, thinking it all depended on me, and instead relying on the Lord for His help in all of life's choices. I now just ask Him to lead while I follow, putting in the effort for what God has for me to do, and then trust Him to work out the problems. The Lord has shown me since my divorce in 1994 that I was to follow His lead, trusting Him for my provisions and care. Now I have given my future to Him and I am looking forward to what He has ahead for me.

Yes, the Lord was taking care of me; and there is no one (or no man) who knows us better nor can meet our needs more fully than our Lord. It is only as we pray asking the Lord for

His healing that we can become whole. A good relationship feels like snuggling up by the fireplace on a chilly night. That is the way that I feel when spending time with my Lord. If He ever was to put that special man into my life, that's the way I want that marriage to feel.☺ Don't you agree?

Now a word of caution to you who may still be an enabler; you are not whole yet, so you will continue to find men who are needy. Remember, *"If a man is broken when you meet him; you are not the one to fix him."* You ladies know what I'm saying, for how many of us can look at a man and see what he could become, with our help, of course.☺ I think many of us are "born fixer-uppers," which is a good quality to have for making a house a home; but not to change your man. **Get rid of that "savior mentality." That job isn't ours; it's God's.**

As I spent more time in my little home with Jesus, the peace I felt was wonderful. I no longer was looking for someone else but had a feeling of contentment. Whether there was to be a relationship with a special man ahead or a work that the Lord has for me to do. Whatever was God's plan I was content just to be His. And, yes, I had known for several years one of God's assignments ahead for me would be to write a book about my journey to encourage you who are still struggling to trust the Lord "totally" with your journeys.

Remember my telling you in the introduction that He had given the title of the book to me about seven years earlier, and this past year He had given me the first seven chapter titles. There was no doubt that the Lord had told me several different times and through three of His people that this was one of my assignments. At this time I knew it was not yet time to begin

144

writing my story. I knew that when He did say, "It's time," He would make a way for me to do it.

A special blessing God gave me during this time was that my retirement money that had been stolen, was not all lost. A lawyer worked with the whole group that had invested with this man. Long story short and about two years later, we recouped about two-thirds of what had been lost. This surprised my friends, even other lawyers, for the recovery in a case like this is rare. **My Heavenly Father was showing how He is the One in control.**

I had been in my little home for over a year now. I enjoyed my first holidays here, even using the clubhouse for my Bible study class Christmas party. My older sister and her husband had flown down in March, bringing my mother with them for a visit. That had been a very special time as it felt good to have family visit me in my home.

The downside during this time was the lack of steady income. The Lord had always blessed that area before, but this time, I could not see the Lord's leading. Could God be punishing me for taking so long to surrender my heart's desire to Him? Was He letting me flounder, showing me what it would be like without Him? No, I didn't believe that for a moment. This first year in my little home had been very good spiritually. It had really been a resting place; God's haven for me as I had learned to trust Him in an area that had been so hard for me to let go of before.

My main job was working in the tour business, which fluctuates a lot. I never knew how many times a month I would work or how much I would make. Unlike when I was to trust

Him for the numbers and income from my social manners business, I worked up to three jobs at a time to keep from spending my savings. But then, there were even times when that was necessary. I believe that the Lord was testing my faith again, not for His sake, but for mine. It was for me to know without a doubt that my trust was not in my solutions, but in God's. I was willing to do whatever job He brought my way for I saw His Hand in them as provisions, but I saw nothing to rely on for the future. When I would feel myself getting up tight over it, I would look up and say, *"My life is in your hands, Lord. If this is where you want me to be, then it's ok with me."*

During this time, one morning I found myself reading Psalm 46. The theme is God is always there to help, providing refuge, security, and peace. **God's power is complete and His ultimate victory is certain. He will not fail to rescue those who love Him.** In the first couple of verses, God's Word tells us that He is our eternal refuge and can give us all of the strength we need for our circumstances. Even though my income was not what I had before, my Heavenly Father would sustain me as long as my focus remained on Him. My heart's desire now was to be all I could be for His glory. For years I had asked the Lord to work through me to reach out to others, but now it was THE desire of my heart that had replaced what "self" had wanted before. **Life may get tough at times, but with God, there is victory.**

At the beginning of this chapter, I wrote a couple of lines from My Utmost For His Highest. *"God takes you through a way that you temporarily do not understand. It is only by going through the spiritual confusion that you will come to understand what God wants for you."* This had been quite a year of becoming content with where God has me in my life. As I look back the Lord had helped me to take that big step from wanting my will to looking forward with excitement to seeing His will worked out in my life. Oh, how I thanked my Lord for His many blessings, and now my heart was longing to see the purpose for which He had been shaping me. The Lord had patiently walked with me on this journey bringing me to this point of total surrender with joy. I heard my voice crying out, "Yes, yes… now I am like the vessel He has asked me to be, emptied of self for the Lord to accomplish His plan."

One morning my devotions were about a lady who had been praying for an answer to a problem and felt that God was saying, "You do it." But all she could see were her own limitations. When it was time to pick up the children, she put on her coat and picked up her limp and lifeless gloves from the table. As she slipped her hands inside allowing them to become useful, she realized God didn't want her to be focused on her limitations, but rather, on His power and enabling. My question had been "How can I write a book? I don't know how!" This illustration was a huge encouragement to me. I realized if telling my story is to bring Him glory, then the Lord would take care of the details. **When God gives us an assignment, it comes with His enablement.**

There is no relationship I can experience that is more fulfilling than the relationship that exists between my Lord and me! Through the years, I have been a construction site that He has been refurbishing. Believe me, there have been many days while on this journey when I have felt the Lord's hammer, chisel and sandpaper while being reshaped.☺ But I also knew it was because He loves me and He wants the best for me, which will be as He works out His plan.

He will deliver us. We will be freed from our past, released from our failures, and challenged by our future. God wants to fill your life with His blessings. Each of us who walks with God walks through storms, winds, and rain, but when we're with Him, we'll be "singing in the rain" for we will feel His sunshine on our faces as He warms our hearts with His magnificent love. This is when life is as good as it gets.

At this time, I feel it is important that I tell you about something that happened to me in the winter of 1998. I was flying home to Houston after a visit to Orlando. This was when I was planning my move back to Florida. The young man who was seated next to me noticed the book I was reading. I don't even remember now what book it was, but it was by a Christian author. He asked if I was a believer. I said, "Yes, are you?" He was, and we introduced ourselves. We had a couple of brief conversations. Then he looked at me the way one does when you want a sincere answer. He asked, "Do you believe that sometimes God tells a believer something to tell another?" That question took me by surprise. But I responded, "Oh, yes, I believe God speaks to us through His Word, through the Holy Spirit, through prayer, and through other believers. Why?" He said, "I have a word for you from God." I have never had a total stranger ever say anything like this to me although I have heard of it happening. I was curious, as he had not volunteered the word yet. So I asked him what God had said? He smiled, saying he didn't have the word yet, but knew God wanted to tell me something. He went back to his reading as I did to mine, although I was not able to concentrate. I wondered, did God have words for me? And if so, what would they be? Just before the pilot announced our approach into Houston, the man touched my arm, smiled and said, "I have your word. ***Go expecting!***" I repeated it and said, "What does that mean?" He said, "I don't know, that's just what God said to give to you." I have pondered these words so many times since. When God shows me something that says, "Go expecting" in something I am reading, or when a pastor says that in his message, I always get a flutter in my stomach. Then it feels like a breeze goes over me. The Lord has encouraged me with those words so many times as I can sense Him saying, ***"Just keep on walking with Me and you will see My best." <u>Go Expecting</u>***!

Now I give these same words to you; "GO EXPECTING."

8

God's Silver Dollar
(His blessing on Our Desires)

*God's Grace! How can we ever understand it? If I had
been in God's shoes and worked all of those years waiting
for my trust to finally be complete in Him, I think I may
have said: "Well, I am glad that you are finally where I've
asked you to be. It sure took you long enough! And since
you have taken so long, it will be just you and me kid.
We'll just cut to the chase and get to work on what I've
had for you to do." ☺*

*I'm most thankful that the Lord's love and grace surpass
our comprehension, aren't you? Oh my, our Lord is so
good and gracious with patience that exceeds any human
ability to understand it.*

I firmly believe that when God knows we desire MORE to be an instrument in His Hands for Him to use for His glory than for any personal desire, this is when He gives us victory. My mind drifts back to something I read in my devotions. **"When the saved soul so trusts Me, his Lord, and seeks no more his own way, he leaves his future in My Hands."** *This was my story and what my praise was about in chapter seven.*

I was now heading into the fall of 2000; and working hard. At this point I had begun to go out on tour jobs that would take me away from my little home for a week at a time. The money was better, but the work meant long hours with very little sleep. I had always felt younger than my years with lots of energy, but at my senior age of fifty-five plus, it was very wearing. Although thankful for the provisions, I knew it was not something I wanted to continue doing for years. More importantly, it surely would not allow me time and energy to work on this book. But then, God knew that. When the time came for me to start my assignment, He would make a way. I was still looking forward to what God's future plan would be. **I was still watching, expecting God's best.**

A couple of my friends had convinced me to join the church choir and sing in the Christmas tree program this year. I didn't know how my work schedule would allow the time for the practices but decided to trust God with that, along with the rest of my life. It turned out to be enjoyable, even with the commitment for lots of practices. So I became one of the ornaments on the tree singing praises to the Lord!

Going to the choir room for one of the first practices, I saw a man whom I had known casually for nearly two years. I had helped with doing the makeup for our Easter program my first year back in Orlando. This man was one of the actors whom I had transformed into his part, by using my palette of makeup and my magic brushes.☺ That had been a time I really enjoyed. I met so many nice people while working with the cast. I already knew a lot of them but some, like this man, I had never met before. He was one of the sweetest men I'd met for a long time. After that, when we would see each other at church, we would throw up our hand and wave, or if we were close enough, we'd give each other a hug. A lot of us from my church are "huggy people" so that was just natural. I knew that he must go to the second church service while I went to the first, because we were always going in opposite directions.

I had seen this man in July when our church had the "Walk through the Bible" conference. I was with friends and in a rush to eat lunch and make it to my next class. When I saw him helping in the lunchroom, I gave him a hug. I asked how he was doing, expecting that same "just fine" answer with the added "how are you?" Instead, he looked sad as he said, "I lost my wife this spring." I knew he was married, but I had never seen them together. I told him I was so sorry, and that was about all I could say. I felt badly for him. I didn't ask any questions at that time, as there were people behind me. Later, I remember reflecting back and noted maybe that was why I hadn't seen him around for a while. Then I saw him about a month later as I was visiting a singles class. He was visiting, too. Now I had only tried the singles' class twice before because I still enjoyed my regular class. They had been family to me for a long time. But because I had tried that class, as I had promised the singles' pastor that I would, Richard now knew that I was single.

After chatting a few times while on my way to the choir room, we did end up making a date. It's funny when I look back on that time. I really thought he wanted to hear more about a business that I was working in and was interested in getting a membership. At first, we said we would meet for coffee. Then before I knew it he was saying, "Do you have any objection to going out for dinner?" Then following my, "Sure, that's fine," I heard myself giving him the directions to my home when he asked if he could pick me up. Whoa…I had just broken my number one rule. Remember? I had always gone to meet a guy for the first date, so I could interrogate him, before having an official date.☺ I had a list of questions that I had begun to ask. Whether he was allowed to pick me up at my place for another date depended on his answers.

The day came for our date. I was a little nervous about breaking my first line of defense rule, because I had found that a lot of the guys in the church weren't much different than the guys of the world. But I had asked a couple of people about him. They said what I had felt. Richard is one of the sweetest guys you will ever know. I was also told that he is a good man. That was important to me. For our first date, we went to a good seafood restaurant close to my little home. We both love good salmon, and that was one of their specialties. As soon as we had ordered our ice teas, I warned him about my list of questions. We both laughed. I'm not sure he knew that I was serious.☺ If I had known how nervous Richard was about this date, I would have been a little easier on him. His son and daughter-in-law told me later how they had sort of coached and encouraged him before our date. We can laugh together about it now. He had been married for forty-one years and I was his first date since he had become a widower.

Remember the statement made to me by my aerobic instructor in Houston? I had questioned if it was "prophetic" at the time. Don't you think the Lord knew what was ahead for me? Now I had forgotten about it until reading my journal while writing this book. However, I did recall another friend saying the same thing to me about six months prior to this date. Both of these ladies felt that God was going to put a man into my life who was a widower after many years of marriage and He would have God's love in his heart for me.

Getting back to the date, the question and answer time went like this. I told him that usually my first question was what church he attended. I already knew the answer, and that he was an active member, not just a bench warmer. I was curious how long he had gone to our church. I was surprised to find that we had begun to go within months of each other in 1985. Both of us were there due to a move into the area about the same time, even coming close to living in the same subdivision. We knew a lot of the same people from church. My Bible study teacher and his wife had known him as long as they have known me, but our paths had never crossed until I did his makeup for the Easter program.

The evening was going well as we enjoyed each other's company. Richard had even noticed that I was left-handed, as he is. We laughed. By now, I was asking him my third question, which was when and how had he given his life to the Lord. Richard responded with, "Now you are getting into my testimony." I said, "Good! I'd love to hear about it." That was the last question he had to answer. He was off the hook! We lingered over the delicious meal as long as we could since we were enjoying our time together. After dinner I told him about a lake nearby with a walk around it and a couple of bridges built over the ends of the lake. It really is a beautiful area. So we decided to go there and walk off some of that dessert we had just eaten. We walked around it a couple of times, then sat on the seats where the concerts were held and talked some more. We had truly enjoyed our time together. When we got back to my little home, Richard said, "How do I sign up for that membership?" I had forgotten all about it, but he hadn't. So I did sell him a membership on our first date.☺

Before long, Thanksgiving was here and I had my ticket to fly home. Richard had hoped I would spend it with him, his kids and their families. I told him that this was a promise I had made to my mother; I would always try to be home for Thanksgiving Day. I didn't know until later from his kids that he was feeling low at their dinner, as I hadn't given him a number to call me. In their words, "daddy was a basket case!" But "Miss Independence" hadn't even thought of doing that. I was used to traveling alone and not having someone checking to see if I was OK.

The next month flew by. Richard and I were spending as much time together as we could. There were the Christmas tree rehearsals and then the programs began for two weeks. My work schedule was lighter during the holidays. I had planned for that. I had been keeping my feelers out for a good job possibility. A friend told me about a lady who said her company was looking for another employee. The job sounded like something I would enjoy so my friend took me to meet her. The job would get me back into the school system selling and delivering books to their libraries and even paid well! Yes, I was interested. While there, I even spoke with her boss. I was excited, as my territory would be with the same schools I had dealt with before when I taught, along with several other schools. Was this the break I had been praying for? Wow, a regular income, and a good one at that! Her boss said we could do the paperwork after the middle of January. I would have close to a month to pray about it to see if this was the Lord's answer for me. I was excited as it sounded good, but no, I was not going to run ahead of God.

Richard and I were getting along great. I continued to get rave reviews from friends who knew him. So many of our friends were asking when we were going to get married. To that I asked, "What happened to the two-year dating rule for us Baptists?" Richard said, "No way, kid, we aren't getting any younger." We knew in our hearts God had put us together. So did our friends. What were we waiting for! One week before Christmas, Richard went with me to my Bible study, and we announced our engagement. My teacher, who knew both of us well, turned around and wrote it on the chalkboard in the praise column. Then everyone applauded! About two weeks prior to this, I'd had lunch with my Bible teacher's wife and another friend of ours. Lynn was teasing me about Richard and me, saying that we were cute together and how she just loved him.

Then she shook her finger at me and said, "Now don't you hurt him." I said, "Wait a minute. You were always protecting me before!"

When I told Richard about the job opportunity, I could sense that he was not really happy about it. His former wife had not worked whereas I had always been a career lady. He thought it sounded like I would be on the road too much, sometimes even being gone overnight. He really didn't like that one! As I was praying I began to see that in becoming his wife I would have my share of responsibilities. Richard and his former wife had adopted one of their grandsons when he was little; he was now fourteen. My nest had been empty for years. Even though I had worked with teenagers for over twenty years, I was sure that alone would be an adjustment for me.

One morning as I was praying, I could sense God saying, *"You have always wanted to be just a housewife, and I have also given you this job of writing about your journey. It's almost time to begin working on it. Your heart's desire for years has been for a good man; one who loves Me and will love you (with My love), cherishing your heart. You were faithful and gave every area of your life to Me. I know that you would be content being with just Me, your Lord. Now that you have joy in your heart, having let go of that heart's desire, I, your Lord have given you that dollar you have prayed for: your heart's desire."* I knew Richard was that man.

The number seven represents God; that had been what chapter 7 was about. The Dollar—God. But did you know the number eight means "new beginnings?" **God was giving me a new beginning!** This is chapter 8. The one God had added.

I told Richard that God had given me a job to do and explained about the book. He was excited. He was also happy I would not be taking the other job. We were married on January 11, 2001. We had a small, but nice wedding in his son's home with just close friends and family. Then we had our celebration reception mid-February. We invited many of our friends and we had a great time. My sisters and their husbands stayed in my condo, since I had put it up for sale and all of my furniture was still in place. They called the condo "Ann's bed & breakfast."☺ While they were there, we showed it to a lady and it was sold!

I am so thankful the Lord has put Richard in my life. Sometimes he will say how blessed he feels that God has put me into his life. To that, I quickly say I am very blessed, too. He is the one God knew would fit my heart's desire. Richard knows that God has given him a tremendous love for me, as he loves me with an adoring love, protects and cares for me. And when the Lord has an assignment for me to do, Richard encourages me to be the best I can be. We are enjoying our "new Beginning!"

This was a busy time for us. We moved my furniture into Richard's house just before the closing on the condo. All three of us were in the Easter program. That first summer we took a nice vacation. As soon as we got home, school was beginning. Richard and I began working on his house to get it ready to sell. Toward the end of August, God said; *"It's time to begin the book."* Later in the fall, we sold Richard's house and were in our new home just one day before our first anniversary. What a year!

ISN'T GOD GOOD TO US? Yes, God has given me my silver dollar!!

My heart's desire is still what it was changed to in chapter seven: to be the vessel my Lord will use for His glory. Richard is quite satisfied to take second place in my heart with God at the top.☺

Only God Knows What Lies Ahead.

Only God knows what lies ahead
I am to trust, knowing I am safe in His Hand
For he has been molding and shaping me, you see
He has had a purpose for which He has been training me.

The testings, the stretchings have been to strengthen my faith.
He has stayed close to lift me, in times
when I thought I would break.
On just a little further, I can hear my Heavenly Father say,
I love you my child, and it's going to be great.

As I see my life unfolding,
I see His provisions, His care and His grace,
And when He is ready to use me,
His love will shine from my face.

For only God knows what lies ahead
I know that I can trust Him, for my Heavenly Father cares.
More than any earthly father can, you see,
As my Heavenly Father prepares what is best for me.

About the Author

GeriAnn Combs is a wife and a mother. She and her husband Richard live in a lovely area just outside Orlando, Florida. Besides her own son, Ann gained two more sons, two daughters and seven grandchildren upon marrying Richard. They are enjoying their home, church, family and friends together as they continue making memories.

With the help of her husband Richard, GeriAnn (Ann) is the founder of a women's ministry called "Caring by Sharing." She is caring for others by sharing her story, to encourage other ladies who are facing tough times and need that encouragement from one who has been there.

Ann was born and raised in mid-western Ohio. Most of her growing up years was spent on a farm, so she and her siblings were no strangers to gardening and farm chores.

Teaching for Ann goes back to her high school years, when she taught baton lessons to 1st through 6th graders. Even before that, Ann was always doing someone else's hair. So her first career was working as a cosmetologist, managing a hair salon for over ten of those twelve years. Her next career sent her back to college to become a teacher for the next sixteen years. Following that career, Ann ran a business, where she taught social manners. As you can see, teaching has been the main title in her varied careers.

Even though Ann was raised in a family who were in church every Sunday, she realized at age "24" that she had not personally accepted Jesus as her Savior and Lord, so that was when her walk with the Lord began. Through her teaching years, her students saw her love for the Lord as she loved and cared for them.

Throughout these years, Ann has had some real difficult times. She has completed this book, entitled "The World's DIMES or God's DOLLARS" which are you seeking? The book is not about money but our choices. It was written not only for you to see a sixteen-year journey in Ann's life, but also to show you God's Faithfulness...giving HOPE to others going through tough times.

Potter's Publishing
P.O. Box 174, 2582 S. Maguire Rd., Ocoee, FL 34761
www.potterspublishing.com